ALBERT EINSTEIN
THE GREATEST MIND IN PHYSICS

Neil Armstrong

Jackie Robinson

Harriet Tubman

Jane Goodall

Albert Einstein

Beyoncé

»TRAILBLAZERS

ALBERT EINSTEIN
THE GREATEST MIND IN PHYSICS

PAUL VIRR

RANDOM HOUSE 🏠 NEW YORK

Text copyright © 2020 by Paul Virr
Cover art copyright © 2020 by Luisa Uribe
Interior illustrations copyright © 2020 by Artful Doodlers
Trailblazers logo design by Mike Burroughs
Additional images used under license from Shutterstock.com

All rights reserved. Published in the United States by Random House Children's Books, a division of Penguin Random House LLC, New York.

Random House and the colophon are registered trademarks of Penguin Random House LLC.

Visit us on the Web! rhcbooks.com

Educators and librarians, for a variety of teaching tools, visit us at
RHTeachersLibrarians.com

Library of Congress Cataloging-in-Publication Data
Name: Virr, Paul, author.
Title: Albert Einstein: the greatest mind in physics / Paul Virr.
Description: New York: Random House Children's Books, [2020] |
Series: Trailblazers | Includes bibliographical references and index.
Identifiers: LCCN 2019031508 | ISBN 978-0-593-12440-6 (trade pbk.) |
ISBN 978-0-593-12441-3 (lib. bdg.) | ISBN 978-0-593-12442-0 (ebook)
Subjects: LCSH: Einstein, Albert, 1879–1955—Juvenile literature. |
Physicists—Biography—Juvenile literature.
Classification: LCC QC16.E5 V57 2020 | DDC 530.092 [B]—dc23

Created by Stripes Publishing Limited, an imprint of the Little Tiger Group

Printed in the United States of America
10 9 8 7 6 5 4 3 2 1

First Edition

Random House Children's Books supports the First Amendment and celebrates the right to read.

Contents

Introduction — 1
Universal Genius

Chapter 1 — 11
Hidden Talents

Chapter 2 — 27
Learning the Hard Way

Chapter 3 — 41
Time to Think

Chapter 4 — 61
Beautiful Ideas

Chapter 5 — 83
Rethinking the Universe

Chapter 6 — 97
Science Superstar

Chapter 7 — 119
After Relativity

Conclusion — 139
Changing the World

Timeline — 152

Further Reading — 156

Glossary — 158

Index — 162

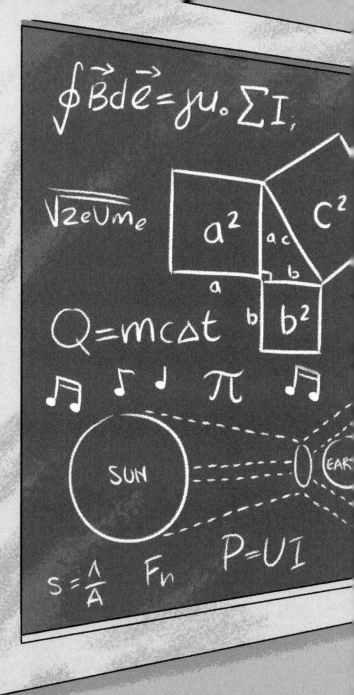

⩳ A NEW UNIVERSE ⩳

On May 29, 1919, two teams of scientists on opposite sides of the Atlantic Ocean were waiting for the sun to disappear. They looked at their watches and nervously scanned the sky for clouds—it was nearly time for an eclipse of the sun to begin! They had traveled all the way from England to South America and Africa, respectively, to take photographs of the stars during this eclipse. These pictures would decide the future of science and would change the life of a physicist named Albert Einstein forever.

Today, most people have heard of Albert Einstein. Even one hundred years after the scientific breakthrough that first put him in the spotlight, he remains a household name. But until this solar eclipse, Einstein was completely unknown outside the scientific community.

That all changed in 1919, just after the end of World War I. The impact of Albert Einstein's new ideas concerning the universe suddenly turned an ordinary professor into one of the most famous and recognizable people ever. Everyone loved his down-to-earth manner, scruffy clothes, and unruly hair. It was his eccentric scientist image, as well as his groundbreaking theory of relativity, that transformed Albert Einstein into the people's scientist—a symbol of genius.

Most people have heard of his theory of relativity, even if they don't know exactly what it is about. Albert Einstein published his theory in 1916, but until 1919 it was unproven by experiment. Relativity was nothing less than a total rethink of the nature of the universe, which it described in just one simple equation. Albert's theory had a small circle of admirers, but other scientists doubted this new idea dreamed up by a young, unknown professor. If relativity was true, it overturned ideas about the universe that had been accepted for centuries!

Galileo Galilei
1564—1642

Einstein didn't invent relativity. He borrowed the basic idea from another genius—Galileo Galilei, an Italian physicist and astronomer. Galileo achieved many things in science, including his early study on gravity and moving objects that the English scientist Isaac Newton built upon later. Galileo described how it was impossible to tell if you were stationary or moving at a constant speed unless you could see yourself relative to something else. The example Galileo used was that if you were belowdecks on a ship and couldn't see out, you might think you weren't moving; but if you were on deck, you would know you were moving, because you could see the shore moving past. This insight would be key to Einstein's theory of relativity.

Isaac Newton
1643—1727

The English scientist and mathematician Isaac Newton discovered the laws of gravity and motion that were accepted for centuries—that is, until Einstein came along. Newton put forward a model of the universe in which everything worked in an orderly and predictable way—a bit like a clockwork mechanism. He described how all the forces and objects in the universe obeyed the same laws. These determined how things moved and interacted in space and time.

Scientists still use Newton's laws to work out the paths of moving objects, from tennis balls to spacecraft orbiting distant planets.

PROVING RELATIVITY

Relativity was a completely new way of explaining how space, time, energy, and matter were all related. It proposed a different way of thinking about gravity. One of the predictions that came out of Albert's theory of relativity was that a huge object with a lot of mass could bend light toward it. To convince everyone that relativity was real, Albert needed to prove his theory with an experiment.

The solar eclipse of 1919 provided the first opportunity for an expedition to test relativity. If the sun *did* bend the light from distant stars, this would prove that matter shapes the space around it and that relativity is correct.

DESTINED FOR FAME?

All of Albert's work over the years had led up to this moment. The solar eclipse would bring together each of the elements involved in his theory in a single event, one that combined light, time, and space. As Albert waited in Berlin, the expedition teams in South America and Africa checked their cameras for the last time. The eclipse was beginning.

Yet it had not always been obvious that Albert was destined for great things. In fact, it was a big surprise to many of his former teachers when they discovered what their pupil had gone on to achieve! For most of them, Albert had been something of a rebel and had shown little sign of genius. Some teachers found him lazy. Just a handful of teachers recognized his unique talents for science and math. But none of them could have imagined the heights that Albert would rise to.

Albert was far from lazy. He was an independent thinker, right from the start. What Albert couldn't learn at school, he simply went and discovered for himself. He loved to read and to talk about science with knowledgeable adults, like his uncle Jakob. Albert's passion for physics began when he was a young boy and was curious about how a magnetic compass worked.

Later, as a student, Albert used his imagination as well as his scientific knowledge to make discoveries about the universe. His amazing ideas didn't come from experiments carried out in a laboratory.

Albert used his mind to explore ideas. He'd ask himself questions, such as "What would you see if it was possible to travel on a beam of light?" Then he'd spend countless hours pondering and picturing solutions to problems like these. Later in his career, he'd go on to say that "Imagination is more important than knowledge."

THE MOMENT OF TRUTH

Five months after the eclipse, the results of the expeditions were announced at a special meeting in London—Einstein's theory of general relativity was finally proved to be correct! It was the kind of exciting story that newspaper reporters needed. World War I had only just ended, and its horrors were still fresh in everyone's minds. People were ready to hear about change, progress, and new ideas.

Almost overnight, Albert Einstein became a global celebrity. Starting in the United Kingdom and the United States, general relativity sparked something in the public imagination. A craze for Einstein and relativity spread like wildfire. Soon the whole world joined the conversation, and journalists were traveling to Berlin to interview the new science superstar.

Even in Germany, where people were occupied with food shortages and hardships following its defeat in the war, Einstein became front-page news.

Albert toured the world and gave talks and lectures that inspired a new generation of scientists. His vivid and visual way of explaining science helped make it more mainstream and people-friendly. Among Albert Einstein's many achievements, perhaps one of the most important is that he remains an inspiration to anyone who dares to think differently or question their world. He modestly summed up his life, saying:

All I have done is ask a few questions.

But as he well knew, questions are just the beginning.

CHAPTER 1

HIDDEN TALENTS

Where does genius begin? Reporters and biographers would look back at Albert Einstein's early years to try to find the first signs of his extraordinary intelligence. But his first few years weren't very remarkable. Albert was born on March 14, 1879, late on a spring morning in his parents' house in the small city of Ulm in southwest Germany. Ulm was an old and beautiful place, standing close to the river Danube. It had an unusual motto, which, when translated from ancient Latin, read roughly as:

> **People from Ulm are mathematicians.**

But even if the city did have a tradition of mathematical excellence, sadly it can't really claim to have had much influence on the genius of Albert Einstein. Only a year later, his family moved!

Albert was born into a respectable middle-class family. His father, Hermann, was the son of a merchant and was trying to make a successful career as a businessman. His mother, Pauline, came from a wealthier family. Albert grew up in a creative home—his father recited poetry aloud, and his mother played piano.

Both their families were Jewish, but Hermann and Pauline were not very religious. They didn't go to the synagogue, and although they followed some of the traditions of the Jewish faith, they were relaxed about others. For instance, they didn't keep kosher, meaning they didn't stick to the strict Jewish rules about food, such as not eating pork.

After three years of marriage, Hermann and Pauline were delighted by the arrival of their first child, a baby boy. Albert was a slightly chubby baby, with a large, oddly shaped head that initially caused some concern. In fact, his mother's first reaction was to declare that his big head and black hair made him look like a monster! Albert's grandmother was similarly shocked, muttering that her grandson was "much too fat!" The family doctor reassured them that the baby was actually quite normal and healthy.

Soon Albert's head took on a more regular shape, so there is no evidence that his genius was due to being born with an unusually large brain! He was a quiet baby and grew up at the center of a loving, tightly knit family, where he was fondly known as "Little Albert."

LITTLE ALBERT

MOVING TO MUNICH

Hermann's brother, Jakob Einstein, was an engineer and an inventor. He had started out working in a gas and plumbing company but was excited by the new electrical industry in Germany. Jakob was ambitious and wanted to be a part of this boom in technology. He suggested to Hermann that they go into the electrical engineering business together. With his technical knowledge and Hermann's business skills, Jakob was sure they would be successful. Ulm was too small for these big ideas, so in the summer of 1880, Hermann moved his family to join Jakob in the large city of Munich.

Hermann's family rented an apartment in the same building where Jakob lived. Later, when the Einstein brothers' new business had gotten well underway, the two families moved next door to each other in the leafier outskirts of the city. It was in this friendly extended household that Albert spent the early part of his childhood. He grew up surrounded by the technical talk of Uncle Jakob and his father, close to the electrical factory that they opened.

Thanks to Pauline, the house was also filled with books and music, so there was no shortage of intellectual stimulation in the world around Little Albert.

Bright Ideas

In the late 19th century, the power of electricity was just beginning to light up the world. In 1879, the year Einstein was born, English inventor Joseph Swan demonstrated an early light bulb that burned for 40 hours. That same year, the American inventor Thomas Edison took out a patent on what would be the first practical commercial light bulb. (A patent protects somebody's invention, so that other people can't take the idea and copy it.) Germany's leaders saw an opportunity with these new technologies. The countr had been in decline following a banking crisis in 1873, so they invested in industries to boost Germany's economy. These included new electrical industries making batteries, electric generators, and machinery.

⋛ A SLOW START ⋚

The Einstein household was a bustling place, filled with comings and goings. But even with all the chatter and activity at home, Albert was a very quiet toddler. While other children his age were starting to learn to speak, he lived in a world of his own and barely said a word. Albert was happy to play with his building blocks for hours on end. Hermann and Pauline thought Albert was too quiet. They started to worry that there might be something wrong with their son.

They called in the family doctor for advice. He thought there was nothing to worry about—Albert was just shy and quiet. Albert rarely spoke until he was about three years old. He later claimed that he hadn't actually wanted to speak. He didn't want to bother with baby talk—he wanted to wait until he had mastered complete sentences!

As a young boy, Albert's speech was slow. He'd practice what he wanted to say under his breath; then he would speak the words out loud. This led the family's maid to conclude that Albert wasn't very smart! However, his grandmother had a different view—she thought Albert was very clever. She was delighted by the amusing things her grandson said. As an adult, when he was asked about his thought process in an interview, Einstein said:

> "I rarely think in words at all. A thought comes—I may try to express it in words afterward."

This visual way of thinking would help Albert come up with his amazing ideas later in life.

≥ NEW TOYS ≤

A year after the Einsteins moved to Munich, there was a new addition to the family—a baby sister for Little Albert! Maja Einstein was born on November 18, 1881. Pauline and Hermann joked with Albert when they first told him about Maja. They said they had a surprise for him, something new to play with. When Albert saw that they meant a little sister instead of a new toy, he cheekily asked, "Where are the wheels?" This might have been an example of the humor that had enchanted his grandmother, or could it have been that he had often seen babies wheeled around in strollers?

Like most brothers and sisters, Maja and Albert would sometimes squabble and fight, but they grew to be very close. Albert was always able to rely on his sister. She would be his best friend all his life.

While Maja was still too small to play with, Albert continued his solitary games. He didn't like toy soldiers, but he loved to make things with building blocks or mechanical construction sets. These toys were perfect for a kid growing up in a household where engineering was a hot topic. Pauline's brother, Caesar Koch, returned from a business trip with another inspiring gift. He gave his nephew a working model of a steam engine. This made such an impression on Albert that he could draw the engine in detail decades later.

One of Albert's favorite games was to build houses from playing cards. Other children, including Albert's younger sister, Maja, could only manage to build a few levels. But Albert would slowly and carefully build cardhouses up to fourteen stories high. The patience required to do this was extraordinary. "It's not that I'm so smart," he once said. "It's just that I stick with problems for longer."

When he was five years old, Albert got sick. While he was recovering in bed, his father gave him a small pocket compass to play with so that he wouldn't be bored. Albert was astonished. The needle of the compass always swung to find north by itself, no matter which way he turned it. Albert was desperate to know how it worked. He had seen how the cogs and wheels in his steam engine fitted together to make things move. But there was no mechanism to make a compass needle move! His father explained it was due to an invisible force called magnetism, but Albert's sense of wonder remained. The little compass left a deep impression on him. It showed Albert for the first time that the world was filled with invisible forces. He realized that "something deeply hidden had to be behind things." His curiosity was awakened. Albert was excited by the thought that all around him, there were secrets waiting to be discovered!

Magnetic Mysteries

Every magnet has two opposite ends, known as the north pole and south pole. If the ends of two magnets are brought close to each other, the north pole of one magnet and south pole of the other magnet will attract each other until they stick together. Two of the same poles push each other away, so a north pole will never stick to another north pole, and the same goes with the south poles.

The invisible force that made the needle of Albert's pocket compass point to north was magnetism. The needle of the compass was actually a magnet, balanced on a mounting so that it could spin freely. Earth has a magnetic field that makes the planet act like a giant magnet. When Albert saw the needle of his compass spinning, it was being pulled to point toward Earth's magnetic north pole.

MUSIC IS BORING!

Around the age of five, Albert developed a temper. When he was angry, his face darkened, and his nose turned white. This was a warning sign to watch out! Sometimes his sister, Maja, would be the target of Albert's fury—he once hit her on the head with a trowel!

Another victim of young Albert's temper was his violin teacher. Unfortunately, Albert did not immediately love music. He found the lessons boring and hated learning scales by heart. At one point, his temper got the better of him. He chased his poor music teacher out of the house, tossing a chair after her as she made her escape!

Albert may have chased away his timid music teacher, but Pauline wasn't going to be easily discouraged. She soon found another violin teacher, one who was tougher and stricter. Music lessons started again. Albert hated music theory, but he often sat down and taught himself to play violin pieces he liked, and even improvised his own music.

Pauline was quietly pleased to see that the seed she had planted had started to grow. Albert was beginning to share her love of music.

CHAPTER 2

LEARNING THE HARD WAY

In 1885, at the age of six, Albert went to school for the first time. There wasn't a Jewish school nearby, so he ended up going to a Catholic elementary school. After a year of one-to-one teaching at home, it was a shock for Albert to suddenly find himself among two thousand other pupils. There were seventy students in Albert's class, but he was the only Jewish one. Albert found it difficult to fit in. He was quiet and dreamy and something of a loner. The teachers treated Albert the same as anybody else, but some of his classmates taunted him for being Jewish.

Albert was different from the other boys. He didn't like to play sports and never joined in with the boys' games in the playground. This made Albert unpopular, as did his habit of always doing his homework! Some of the boys were mean—they gave him a German nickname that meant "Goody Two-shoes."

At the end of his first year, Albert was top of his class. He brought home a glowing school report, and his parents were delighted.

But Albert was unhappy with the teaching at school. He found it slow and boring. Repetition and learning facts by heart took the place of thinking for yourself. Albert wanted to learn in the most direct way possible.

As well as being disappointed with the teaching, Albert had problems getting along with the other boys. Being an outsider made him a target for bullies. The twenty-minute walk home from school became a nightmare. Albert regularly faced anti-Semitic insults and even physical attacks, just because he was a Jew.

Anti-Semitism

Hostility toward Jews is known as anti-Semitism. This type of racism was common in Germany and many other countries when Albert Einstein was a boy. Jewish people were viewed with distrust and were subject to laws that restricted their freedom. Sometimes they were forced to live in separate areas of cities called ghettos.

MILITARY-MINDED

Unfortunately, school life got even worse for Albert. In the autumn of 1888, just before he was ten years old, he moved to the Luitpold Gymnasium, a kind of high school in Germany. Albert found his new school very strict. The teachers expected their pupils to obey without question, like soldiers in an army. In fact, Albert would scornfully refer to his teachers as "drill sergeants" and "lieutenants." Learning was mainly repeating and memorizing facts. Nobody dared to challenge the textbooks or to question the teachers.

He saw that strict rules controlled life outside school, too. At that time, all young men in the new German Empire had to become soldiers for three years of military service. Albert once encountered a military parade while he was out with his parents. The soldiers were marching perfectly in step with each other, and their uniforms made them all look the same. Albert was so disturbed by the sight that he burst into tears. "When I grow up, I don't want to be like those poor people!" he cried to his parents. Albert's dislike of soldiers and aggression would later grow into pacifism, a total rejection of war and violence.

The German Empire

Germany was still a new country when Albert Einstein was a boy. The 25 independent states that made up the new German Empire had only joined together in 1871. Led by the emperor Wilhelm II,

WILHELM II

and under the guidance of Chancellor Otto von Bismarck, Germany rapidly industrialized. Its cities—including Munich, where Albert lived—expanded with workers. Along with industrialization, Germany built up its navy and army so that it could expand its empire overseas.

OTTO VON BISMARCK

REBEL WITH A SMILE

Albert soon started to rebel against the rigid rules of his school. He sat right at the back of the class, smiling to himself as if he was amused by some private joke. This slowly unnerved one teacher, who angrily told him off. Albert mock-innocently asked, "But what have I done?" The teacher stiffly answered:

> "Your mere presence here undermines the class's respect for me."

Some of the other teachers also thought Albert was lazy and rude. But he excelled at math and science, and even did well in Latin and ancient Greek, both of which he didn't really see the point of learning. Albert's rebellious attitude blinded some of his teachers to his intelligence. Albert's casual manner and confidence came across as arrogance and rubbed people the wrong way.

MONDAY	TUESDAY	WEDNESDAY	THURSDAY	FRIDAY
Latin	Ancient Greek	Latin	Ancient Greek	Latin
German	Latin	French	French	Latin
Mathematics	Latin	Mathematics	Geography	Mathematics
Geography	Ancient Greek	Science	Latin	Ancient Greek
Ancient Greek	Geography	Latin	German	Ancient Greek
Science	German	French	Mathematics	German

What's the point?

But no physics? I have to wait until seventh grade? No way!

⋝ SACRED GEOMETRY ⋜

School couldn't keep pace with Albert's curiosity. Frustrated by his lessons, he decided to teach himself at home by reading in his spare time. Luckily, Albert had some inspiring and smart people close by to help him.

First was his uncle Jakob. He encouraged Albert's love of mathematics and taught him the basics of algebra. Jakob was an imaginative teacher and turned what could have been a dusty old schoolbook lesson into a fun game. He had Albert imagine that he was hunting an unknown mathematical beast called X. To catch X and win the game, Albert had to find its numerical value in an algebraic equation.

Jakob gave his nephew a book on math that Albert later described as a "sacred little geometry book." This introduced Albert to classical Greek geometry, a branch of math that is all about shapes and their properties, and includes the theorems of Euclid and Pythagoras. Albert loved the simplicity and logic of geometry. Of course, he insisted on working out his own proof of Pythagoras's theorem! He described the discovery of geometry as a "second wonder" to add to that first wonder of seeing the pocket compass.

⩾ POPULAR SCIENCE ⩽

The second inspiring figure to enter Einstein's life was a Jewish medical student named Max Talmud. In keeping with a Jewish tradition where a poor scholar was invited to share a meal with the family, Albert's parents invited Max to lunch once a week. Max was more than ten years older than Albert, but they hit it off right away and became good friends. They both loved to share ideas. When Max visited on Thursdays, he would bring popular science books with him. With Germany at the cutting edge of science and technology, there was a huge public interest in science. Popular science books were written for this audience and became bestsellers. Albert would devour the books Max brought from cover to cover. Conversations about science, math, and philosophy with Max were much more interesting than anything taught at school!

Max instantly realized that Albert was extremely clever, but he worried about his young friend. He never saw Albert play with children his own age. Albert seemed happier exploring the complex world of science. In fact, Max never saw Albert read anything but the most challenging books!

Max did his best to answer Albert's endless questions, but he was humble enough to admit that the young scientist's knowledge soon outstripped his own.

"The flight of Albert's mathematical genius was so high that I could no longer follow." —Max Talmud

MARVELOUS MOZART

Suddenly, following an unpromising start, Albert's violin playing got a boost. He discovered the music of Mozart! It was only then that something clicked for the budding musician. Albert later admitted, "I really only started to learn when I was about thirteen years old, after I had fallen in love with Mozart's sonatas." Because he wanted to play them himself, Albert had to improve his violin technique. It was the start of a lifelong passion for playing music.

Albert's violin playing had improved so much by the time he was sixteen that he got a special mention from a school inspector. The inspector wrote that Einstein's emotional performance of a Beethoven sonata had "sparkled." But it was Mozart rather than Beethoven whom Albert appreciated the most—he felt a sense of wonder and mystery when listening to his music. It was similar to the feeling of seeing into hidden things that he had experienced with the pocket compass. Albert described Mozart's music as being "so pure and beautiful that I see it as a reflection of the inner beauty of the universe."

Wolfgang Amadeus Mozart
1756—1791

The 18th-century composer Mozart was born in Salzburg, Austria. He was a musical prodigy who started composing when he was just five years old! As a child, he wowed crowds—sometimes even royalty—with his performances on keyboard instruments and the violin. In his short lifetime, he composed more than 600 works, including the sonatas that Einstein loved so dearly.

WOLFGANG AMADEUS MOZART

MUSIC FOR LIFE

In the late 19th and early 20th centuries, before television, smartphones, and the internet, people often made their own entertainment. Playing music at social gatherings was common. There was a lot of music making in Albert's family home, with regular musical evenings. He played solo party pieces but also duets, with his mother, Pauline, accompanying him on the piano.

Albert played violin most of his life. Music became entwined with his studies. While working alone, he'd often break off to play on the violin or piano for a spell. Then he'd return to the theoretical problem he was wrestling with. Music also helped him relax after a hard day's work. A visitor recalled Albert unwinding in the kitchen of his Berlin apartment by improvising on violin. As an adult, Albert said in an interview, "If I were not a physicist, I would probably be a musician."

When he was famous and traveled around the world, Albert always took his beloved violin with him. He'd play in public at parties and events with all kinds of musicians, from amateurs to famous soloists. But though Albert was a good player, he wasn't a genius on the violin!

An expert violinist who played with him joked about Albert's questionable timing, saying, "What's the matter, professor, can't you count?" Even if some were critical of his technique, everyone who saw Albert play agreed that his performances were always emotional.

LOSING HIS RELIGION

One in twenty of the pupils at the Luitpold Gymnasium was a Jew, so there was some teaching of the Jewish religion at the school. Inspired by his religious-studies teacher, Albert had a brief religious phase. He stopped eating pork and eagerly read the Old Testament. He even started preparing for his bar mitzvah, when he would become part of Munich's Jewish community. His parents were mildly surprised but supportive. However, Albert's enthusiasm for traditional religion didn't last long. His growing scientific knowledge soon led him to the conclusion that "much in the stories of the Bible could not be true." What's more, Albert felt that the religious teaching at school had set out to deliberately mislead pupils. This strengthened his distrust of authority.

CHAPTER 3

TIME TO THINK

Albert grew increasingly frustrated with the "mindless and mechanical" teaching at school. He responded by switching his efforts to more private study at home. While other children his age were outdoors playing, Albert sat indoors, poring over the pages of books or trying out math problems. While he studied, Albert could sometimes hear soldiers marching through the streets. But he didn't let their heavy footfalls distract him. Life in Munich, just like school with its uniforms and rules, was becoming more regimented, but in the world of his thoughts, Albert was free to be himself.

In what Albert called "private study," he found the excitement that was missing at school. Albert loved to wrestle with a theoretical question and would spend hours lost in thought, trying out different solutions. When he was thinking, the world and all his everyday troubles disappeared. Albert's sister, Maja, once noticed her older brother at a noisy family gathering. While everyone else was chatting and having fun, Albert lay on the sofa. He had balanced his inkwell close by and was scribbling on a piece of paper. Albert was in a world of his own. Maja said that Albert could "engross himself in a

problem so much that noise stimulated rather than disturbed him."

Albert explored the subjects that interested him most, such as science and mathematics. He worked through books of geometry problems at lightning speed, which amazed his friend Max. While lessons at school plodded along, Albert raced ahead in his spare time. He covered the whole of his school's mathematics program in just a year! Meanwhile, in class Albert didn't bother with subjects he found boring. He rarely handed in any assignments for subjects like ancient Greek!

BIG CHANGES

In 1893, when Albert was fifteen years old, the Einsteins' electrical business suffered a catastrophic blow. They had put all their hopes on winning a major contract to install electric lighting in the center of Munich but lost out to a larger company. Without the contract, there wasn't enough work. Hermann and Jakob were forced to close their business. They decided to relocate and start again in Italy.

In a short time, Albert saw his stable family life completely swept away. The family business was broken up and sold to pay its debts. Then the home he had grown up in was sold. A property developer demolished it to make way for a new apartment block. Albert later wrote about these painful experiences. He described how he and Maja had "watched the destruction of their fondest memories."

Albert also saw firsthand the effect this business disaster had on his father. Hermann was worn out and deeply disappointed. He had worked hard, but his hard work hadn't been enough. There was also a dark suspicion that prejudice against Jews had played a part in the brothers' failure to win the contract.

This injustice, whether real or imagined, deepened Albert's dislike of Germany. It also led him to reject the competitiveness of business. Albert was an idealistic teenager—he had higher goals than making money.

⋛ LEFT BEHIND ⋚

Just when Albert thought things couldn't get any worse, they did. Rather than take Albert with them to Italy, his parents decided it would be better if he remained in Munich to finish the last three years of high school! Pauline and Hermann arranged for Albert to stay in a boardinghouse. A distant relation who lived in Munich had promised to keep an eye on him. Albert was far from happy with this arrangement. He hated school, he hated Munich, he hated Germany, and he certainly didn't want to live with strangers. But Albert was fifteen, and he had no choice but to do as his parents said . . . at least for now!

In 1894, Pauline and Hermann moved to Milan in the north of Italy, taking Maja with them. Albert's dearest friend, Max, had also left Munich, sailing to America to work in a hospital in New York. As for school, Albert hadn't made any real friends there. He was completely alone.

Albert continued with school, but it was becoming unbearable. He was always getting into trouble with his super-strict teachers. In letters to his family, Albert seemed his normal self, but the truth was that he was lonely and unhappy.

After six months of living alone in Munich, Albert knew he couldn't take any more. His problems at school had reached crisis point, and he was now also worried that he'd have to do military service if he stayed in Germany any longer.

The letters he got from his family made it even worse—they described their new life in Italy and made it sound like a sunny paradise compared to Munich! Albert's parents had been very firm about the need for him to finish his education in Germany, but Albert had reached his limit. He came up with a clever plan to break free!

POSTCARD

AIR MAIL

Dear Albert,

We miss you dearly and wish you were here!

With love
xxx

Mr Albert Einst

Munich

Germany

First, Albert went to see Bernard Talmud, his friend Max's brother. Bernard was a doctor. When he heard Albert's story, Bernard was convinced to sign a medical certificate. He wrote that Albert was on the verge of a nervous breakdown and that he should leave school for the sake of his health.

Next, Albert went to see his mathematics teacher, Joseph Ducrue. Unlike some of the other teachers at the Luitpold Gymnasium, Joseph Ducrue had a very high opinion of Albert. His star pupil persuaded him to write a letter. It said that Albert's knowledge of math had already reached the level expected of a graduate. This was clever forward-thinking on Albert's part. If he quit school before graduating, Albert knew he'd need evidence of his talents in order to continue his studies somewhere else.

What happened next is not completely clear. Either Albert was summoned to the office of his Greek teacher, Dr. Degenhart, or he marched in himself, armed with Bernard's medical certificate. Their conversation was brief. Albert asked to be released from school, and Dr. Degenhart replied by telling Albert he was being expelled! This was just what Albert wanted.

There could be no going back from here. The only problem now was his parents....

> Luitpold-Gymnasium,
> 1894
>
> To whom it may concern,
>
> This is to certify that Albert Einstein has been a pupil of mine in mathematics at the Luitpold-Gymnasium and that I consider him to be an exceptional student. His level of understanding of the subject is that of a graduate.
>
> Yours sincerely,
> Joseph Ducrue

⋛ FREE AT LAST ⋛

In December 1894, Albert's parents got a shock—Albert suddenly showed up on their doorstep in Italy! They were very upset. It looked as if Albert had thrown away his academic future by leaving school with no qualifications. At first they wanted him to return to Munich. But when they heard how unhappy he had been, they relented. They decided to make the best of the situation and started to explore Albert's educational options. In the meantime, Albert enjoyed his newly won freedom. He went walking in the mountains and visited churches, museums, and art galleries. He found the Italians friendlier than people in Munich. Albert was happy for the first time in ages.

The happy months of my stay in Italy are my most beautiful memories.

⋛ A FRESH START ⋚

Luckily, there was a way for Albert to return to higher education. The Zurich Polytechnic—a college in neighboring Switzerland that offered courses in practical subjects, such as engineering—accepted students who hadn't been to high school. All Albert needed to do was pass an entrance exam. It was decided that Albert would study there to become a math and physics teacher. Hermann was happy that his son would be studying a practical, work-related subject rather than daydreaming about theories. Albert was glad to have escaped Germany. He started the process of giving up his German citizenship.

While studying for the exam, Albert helped Uncle Jakob at the new factory. He impressed everyone by wandering into the office one morning and casually solving a mechanical problem that Jakob and his head engineer had been struggling with for days. Albert found a way to fix their machine in just fifteen minutes! He also wrote his first physics essay, which he proudly sent to his uncle Caesar Koch. It was about the ether, a theoretical invisible medium that light was thought to travel through. His essay wasn't groundbreaking, but the subject was one that Einstein would return to later with astounding effect.

Unfortunately, there was a problem with the Zurich Polytechnic plan—you had to be eighteen years old to take the entrance exam, and Albert was just sixteen. His parents asked an influential friend to plead Albert's case with the principal of the Polytechnic. The letter from Albert's math teacher saved the day, convincing the principal that Albert was a gifted student and would be mature enough to study at the Polytechnic.

In October 1895, Albert confidently caught the train to Zurich to take the exam. But his confidence was misplaced—Albert did really well on the science questions, but he failed the general-knowledge section! Thankfully, the principal of the Polytechnic could see the potential in this young scientist. He advised Albert to return after he had spent a year filling in the gaps in his education.

THE LUMINIFEROUS ETHER

When Albert wrote his first physics essay, the existence of the ether was taken for granted. Just as waves travel through water, scientists had proposed that there was a medium that light traveled through, called the ether. How else did it get through the vacuum of space from the sun to Earth? The only problem was that nobody had been able to find the ether! This incredible substance supposedly filled all of space yet was completely invisible. Two American scientists, Albert Michelson and Edward Morley, had cast doubt over the existence of the ether with an experiment in 1887. Albert would eventually come up with a theory that got rid of the ether once and for all.

Back in my day, we called the ether the fifth element!

ARISTOTLE 384–322 BCE

BACK TO SCHOOL

Albert started at the Aarau school in Zurich in the fall of 1895. He was sixteen and had perfected a striking rebellious look. Albert wore a battered gray felt hat, tipped back on top of his wayward black hair. He was scruffy and likable and fit in well with the relaxed atmosphere of the school. One of his classmates described him as a "laughing philosopher" who was "unconfined by conventional restrictions." The teaching style at Aarau was completely different from the approach at his previous school. The Aarau

teachers encouraged observation and the use of thought experiments to work through ideas rather than memorizing information.

Thought Experiments

A thought experiment is a way of solving a problem or exploring a scientific question using only imagination. Visualizing various possible outcomes can be just as useful as an actual experiment. For instance, you could picture flaws in a theory that might disprove it. Thought experiments had been around for centuries, and there were many examples in classical Greek science and philosophy. Galileo also famously used a thought experiment to work out his ideas about gravity.

Now, at the age of sixteen, Albert began the thought experiment that would lead him to relativity. What would it be like if you could run just as fast as a beam of light? What would you see if you looked at it? Would the light wave freeze and seem to stand still?

≥ REBEL SCIENTIST ≤

Albert passed his exams at Aarau with exceptional grades and, at the age of seventeen, became the youngest student to enter the Zurich Polytechnic. A rich aunt gave him an allowance to help him study, as Albert's parents were struggling financially.

It didn't take long before Albert's personality made its mark. Soon he was up to his old tricks, skipping lectures and annoying the professors with his attitude. Albert was disappointed that physics was only a small part of the program. He found some of the teaching out of date, especially when compared to the exciting ideas he was reading about in his spare time. Before long, Albert was spending most of his time studying the "masters of theoretical physics" at home. He borrowed lecture notes from his friend Marcel Grossmann to catch up, but Albert's absence was noticed by his teachers. It even led to the mathematics professor describing Albert as a "lazy dog."

But Albert was never lazy. Whenever he got the chance, he would talk about physics or philosophy. Around this time, Albert met Michele Besso at a musical evening. It was the start of a lifelong friendship. Conversations with Michele helped shape Albert's ideas.

Theoretical physics is a branch of science that uses math to try to explain the world around us and predict what might happen in the future. It creates models that help us visualize and understand the behavior of things in complex systems—like the universe!

Albert loved theoretical physics, but he also enjoyed practical experiments and working in the laboratory. However, his tendency to push things to the limit backfired one day, and he blew up one of his experiments!

Albert hurt his hand so badly that he couldn't play violin for a spell. Even worse, he got the lowest grade possible from the professor in charge of practical lessons, who told Albert he was "hopeless at physics."

LOVE AND SCIENCE

Albert wasn't the only outsider at the Poly with a passion for pure science. Mileva Marić was the sole female student studying mathematics and physics. It was a sign of Mileva's dedication to science that she had broken into this male-dominated field and had won a place at the Zurich Polytechnic. It wasn't long before the two outsiders became friends, and soon after, Albert and Mileva fell in love. The couple had very similar interests. They studied together, shared their textbooks, and spent hours bouncing ideas off each other. Albert enjoyed the company of someone as "strong and independent" as he was. They grew closer and planned to marry, but Albert's mother didn't think Mileva would be a suitable wife for her son. Mileva was clever and unconventional—as a female scientist she didn't fit in with Pauline's ideal of the traditional German housewife. Despite this hostility, Albert and Mileva grew closer. They prepared for their exams together and made plans for their future.

In the summer of 1900, Albert and Mileva got their exam results. Albert wasn't the top of his class as he had been the year before, but he scraped through with a pass and was now a qualified teacher. Sadly, Mileva, who had excelled at all her previous studies, failed for the very first time in her life. The moment had come for Albert and Mileva to make some big decisions. A new century was beginning, and the young couple would face it together.

CHAPTER 4

BEAUTIFUL IDEAS

In 1901, five years after he had given up his German nationality, twenty-one-year-old Albert was finally granted Swiss citizenship. The paperwork had been difficult, and it had cost almost all his savings, but it was worth it. Now that he was a citizen, he could stay in Switzerland and find a job. Albert needed money; he wanted to marry Mileva and set up a home with her. His rich aunt had stopped sending money to support him since he had finished his studies. Albert couldn't ask his parents for help, because his father's business wasn't doing very well. Besides, his mother was completely against his marrying Mileva. There was only one thing to do, and that was to find a teaching job—right away!

FEELING REJECTED

Albert had his diploma, but finding a permanent teaching job was more difficult than he'd expected. He tried to get a teaching assistant position at the Zurich Polytechnic, where some of his former classmates were already working. Unfortunately, the professors remembered Albert all too well—as the disrespectful student who had rarely shown up for their classes! They turned Albert down and were reluctant to recommend him for other jobs.

Mileva and Albert struggled for money and took whatever work they could find. They were both employed as private tutors, and Albert occasionally found short-term work as a substitute teacher. Albert described their situation in a letter:

> Neither of us has a job, and we support ourselves by private lessons—when we can pick up some.

Albert wrote letters offering his services to every university he could think of. But each job application he sent was rejected. Albert was disheartened. Hermann tried to help his son by writing a letter to the famous German chemist Wilhelm Ostwald. Hermann asked him to give Albert a chance as his assistant. But neither Ostwald nor any of the professors that Albert had written to could see his potential. It was a tough time for Albert, and he felt miserable and disillusioned.

⋛ A LUCKY BREAK ⋚

Albert wanted to marry Mileva, but his mother was still set against the idea. She wanted Albert to break off the relationship and told him that marrying Mileva would ruin his career prospects. But Albert loved Mileva and was determined to marry her—if only he could get a job! Then, in late 1901, Marcel Grossman, Albert's friend and classmate from the Zurich Poly, came to the rescue. He had recommended Albert for a permanent job at the Swiss patent office in Bern. This was where inventors sent their plans to be checked. If their inventions worked and were original, they would be granted a patent to protect their ideas.

A job checking scientific ideas and inventions sounded ideal to Albert, and he jumped at the chance. He was so keen that he moved to a cheap room in Bern to prepare for the interview. Money was tight, so while he waited to be called by the patent office, he got some more teaching work as a private tutor. It was tough being apart from Mileva, but Albert knew this "wonderful job" was his big chance.

Finally, in May 1902, Albert was invited for an interview with Friedrich Haller, the director of the patent office.

He was impressed with Albert's technical knowledge. Haller also saw that Albert's family background in electrical engineering could be very useful. Many of the new inventions that came to the office for approval were electrical products. He thought Albert was perfect for the job. Haller shook the young graduate's hand and offered him the position right away. Albert was delighted. His money worries were over—now he could marry his beloved Mileva!

Lieserl

Unknown to Albert's family, Mileva and Albert had a baby daughter in 1902. Mileva went home to Hungary to have the baby—in those days, it was frowned upon to have a child outside of marriage. They named her Lieserl, but sadly Albert never got to meet his daughter. There are no official records, but it is likely that Lieserl either died or was given up for adoption when she was just a few months old.

A DEATH IN THE FAMILY

Just after Albert started work, he had some bad news. His father had suffered a heart attack. Albert caught a train to Milan and rushed to Hermann's bedside. It was a terrible shock to see his father so ill at only fifty-five years old. Albert thought that the strain of work was to blame. Hermann was pleased to see his son, but very unhappy that disagreements about Mileva had caused a rift between Albert and his mother. To heal the division in his family, Hermann gave his blessing to Albert and Mileva's marriage, and Pauline finally relented. On October 10, 1902, shortly after Albert's arrival, Hermann Einstein died. Albert was deeply upset.

MARRIED AT LAST

In January 1903, Albert and Mileva got married in Bern. It was a small wedding. Neither of their families came, but they celebrated with friends. They returned late to Albert's lodgings, but he had forgotten the key. It was typical of absentminded Albert—they had to wake up the poor landlord to let them in!

At last, it seemed that Albert's efforts had been worthwhile. He had a well-paying job, he was married, and he had Mileva and a network of friends to share his ideas with. With some of these friends he formed a small club that met for intellectual discussions. They called it the Olympia Academy. Even better, in 1904, Albert had managed to get Michele Besso, his dear friend from the Zurich Polytechnic, a job at the patent office, too. Albert described Michele as the best person in Europe to bounce ideas off. The pair often discussed Albert's theories during long walks around Bern.

Just over a year after they had married, Mileva gave birth to a son. They named him Hans Albert Einstein. Mileva took care of their newborn and ran the house while Albert worked at the patent office.

BEAUTIFUL IDEAS

Albert's job at the patent office turned out to be ideal. He worked in a grand building close to the center of Bern. As a technical expert third class, Albert checked the patent applications for new inventions. First, he had to pore over the blueprints and technical information to check that the invention worked. Then he also had to check that it hadn't already been invented and patented by someone else!

Some patents made a good starting point for a thought experiment. One of the inventions Albert had to check was designed to keep clocks at railway stations telling the same time. Food for thought for a scientist interested in the problem of space, time, and how different people might experience them.

Each patent was a problem waiting to be solved, just like the geometry problems that had fascinated Albert as a boy. His office had the atmosphere of a library, and once Albert had learned the basics, he found his new job easy and even stimulating. Albert later said that the patent office was the place "where I hatched my most beautiful ideas."

In 1900, the British physicist Lord Kelvin had declared:

> "There is nothing new to be discovered in physics now."

Just five years later, Albert Einstein, an unknown twenty-six-year-old patent clerk, was about to prove him wrong. Albert didn't have a laboratory or access to an academic library, but that didn't hold him back. In fact, working alone meant he could think more freely than he would have been allowed in a stuffy traditional university. Albert worked things out for himself and used his visual imagination to think in a way that nobody else had dared. He'd scribble ideas down at work on scraps of paper. Later he would talk excitedly with his friends about his most recent breakthroughs or disappointments. In the evenings, he would write up his beautiful ideas and started to prepare them for publication. The results of his thought experiments were astounding and totally original. In 1905, Albert presented them in a flurry of articles that would shake up the world of theoretical physics.

EINSTEIN'S ARTICLES

In March 1905, Albert sent an article about the nature of light to the famous German journal *Annalen der Physik*. Albert showed how light could behave as a stream of particles as well as a wave. He wrote to one of his friends from the Olympia Academy, describing his article as "very revolutionary."

What Is Light?

For centuries, scientists had argued about what light actually was. When you heat an iron poker, some of the heat energy is turned into light. As the poker gets hotter, it glows red, orange, and then white. German physicist Max Planck was interested in how energy, temperature, and the color of heated objects are related. He discovered that energy doesn't flow steadily but is transferred in specific packets, each of which is called a quantum (plural: quanta).

Max couldn't figure out why. That was where Albert came in.

Albert explained how the specific colors produced by hot objects are due to light acting as a stream of particles. Each particle or quantum of light carries a specific packet of energy. The higher the frequency of the light, the bigger the packet of energy. Each frequency corresponds to a different color.

Albert's paper on light energy was an astonishing achievement. Then, just a couple of months later, he followed it with two additional groundbreaking papers about molecules and how they move. At that time, the existence of atoms was still theoretical, even though the idea had been around since the ancient Greeks. Albert's article for *Annalen der Physik* proved that they exist—and even calculated how big they are!

In 1827, a Scottish botanist named Robert Brown had looked through a microscope at grains of pollen in water. He saw them randomly moving around, an effect that became known as Brownian motion, named after its discoverer. Albert used statistics to show how the combined forces of individual water molecules jostling around could make pollen grains zigzag about. Albert then used some clever math to work out the size of water molecules. He submitted this paper, titled *A New Determination of Molecular Size*, to the University of Zurich to earn his PhD, but it was rejected for being too short!

A New Determination of Molecular Size
By Albert Einstein

THE kinetic theory of gases made possible the earliest determinations of the actual dimensions of the molecules, whilst physical phenomena observable in liquids have not, up to the present, served for the calculation of molecular

REJECTED

Albert shrugged his shoulders, added an extra sentence, and submitted it again the following year—this time it was accepted. Albert received his doctorate from the University of Zurich in 1906 and was finally Dr. Einstein.

SPECIAL RELATIVITY

For his fourth paper, Albert returned to one of his favorite topics—light. He recalled his youthful thought experiment about riding on a beam of light. If he was traveling at the speed of light, would the other light waves around him seem to stand still?

While riding a tram to work, Albert looked back at the old clock tower in Bern's city center and imagined his tram car traveling at the speed of light. He realized this would mean the light from the clock face wouldn't be able to catch up with him, so its hands would remain frozen. Time would stop. At least it would for him, if he was using the clock tower to figure out if he was going to be late for work! Yet the hands on his watch would move around as they usually did—and for people back at the clock tower, time would continue in the normal way. Albert realized that time could pass differently depending on how fast you were traveling. For Newton, time was absolute and ticked along the same everywhere. Now Albert had a hunch that time wasn't the same for everyone. Later that day, he went for a long walk with Michele Besso to talk his ideas over.

The next day, Albert saw it all clearly. He realized that the faster you move through space, the slower you move through time. Light is the only constant, moving along at the same speed. But time isn't fixed—it can stretch and shrink! This effect, known as time dilation, means that there is no absolute time; everybody has their own personal version of time. Albert wrote to Michele:

I've completely solved the problem. My solution was to analyze the concept of time.

Time cannot be absolutely defined.

Albert's new model of the universe was mind-bendingly different. According to his model, the faster you travel, the more slowly time passes for you. Which means that if one twin zooms around space at high speed and returns to Earth, he will have aged less than his brother! Similarly, if you place identical clocks at the equator and the North Pole, they will tell slightly different times.

Time for Twins

1. Twin one sets off into space. Twin two stays behind.

2. Time passes—but due to relativity, not at the same rate!

3. Twin one returns to Earth to discover that twin two is older. But that's impossible, isn't it?

It wasn't just time that Albert discovered was relative; it was distance, too. Objects change shape and get shorter the faster they hurtle toward you. All these differences are very tiny for people in the everyday world, but as objects move closer to the speed of light, the differences become more significant.

People needed a new way of looking at things to grasp Albert's universe of flexible space-time! He gave his paper the not-so-catchy title *On the Electrodynamics of Moving Bodies*, but later he would refer to it more simply as "special relativity." This was because the theory described a very special situation, one limited to objects moving steadily in straight lines. Albert knew the universe was more complicated than that and realized he had more work to do on relativity.

It took Albert just six weeks to work out his theory, but it overturned ideas about the universe that had seemed certain for two centuries. Einstein had made a great leap forward in scientific thinking. Now the rest of the world would have to catch up with him!

The Famous Equation

As if special relativity wasn't enough to make 1905 a year of scientific miracles, Albert finished by writing a short paper about energy and mass. In this almost casual postscript to special relativity, Albert noted how energy and mass are essentially the same—they can be converted into each other. This brief afterthought included the first version of the now-famous equation:

$$E = mc^2$$

E is energy, *m* is mass,
and *c* is the speed of light.

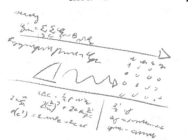

Albert's equation revealed how vast amounts of energy could be released from tiny amounts of matter. He had just described the source of the nuclear power that lights up the stars.

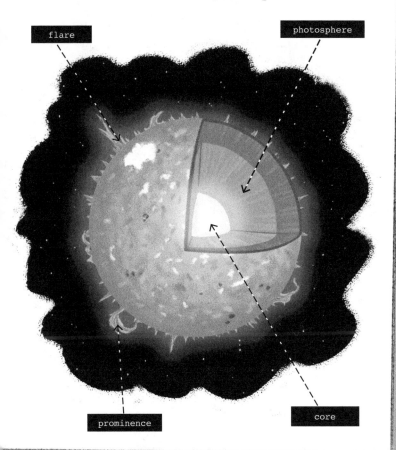

Albert knew that he had achieved something remarkable in the space of less than a year. It had been an incredible feat of thought, imagination, and hard work. He later described what was going on in his brain that year and said it was as if "a storm broke loose in my mind." Having submitted his articles, Albert waited for the world to sit up and take notice. His sister, Maja, said:

> "Albert thought that being published in famous, widely read journals would immediately get everyone's attention."

But there was no instant acclaim. In fact, as the weeks passed, the silence became deafening.

CHAPTER 5

RETHINKING THE UNIVERSE

Albert was exhausted. He had worked extremely hard to finish his articles while also holding down a day job at the patent office. It had been an intense burst of effort. It's no surprise that afterward, Albert took to his bed and slept for the better part of two weeks! When he had recovered his strength, he simply carried on with his work and home life just as before.

Albert divided his daily routine into three parts. He worked for eight hours at the patent office, then did eight hours of his own science work before turning in for eight hours of sleep. The problem was that sometimes Albert cut back on sleep to carry on scribbling equations and working on his theories.

Albert was surprised that his articles hadn't gotten a reaction from other scientists. But at least he had his job to take his mind off the disappointment. Ever since his school days, Albert had been easily bored, but he wasn't bored by his job as a patent clerk. He enjoyed the variety of his work. Every day was different, with new inventions to check. Albert's boss, Friedrich Haller, was pleased with his progress. In April 1906, he gave Albert a pay raise and promoted him to technical expert second class. The extra money came in handy. Ever since the death of his father, Albert had been sending money to his mother. Unfortunately, Hermann hadn't been a very good businessman—Pauline had been left with many debts that needed repaying.

THE FOURTH DIMENSION

Slowly Albert's articles in *Annalen der Physik* began to get noticed. In 1906, he proudly wrote to a friend that his work was finally "meeting with much acknowledgment." Albert's ideas were so new that they took time to sink in. But when they did, they made a big impression. One of the first to grasp what Albert had achieved was the famous theoretical physicist Max Planck. Albert's theory of special relativity had instantly caught his "lively attention." Planck got in touch with Albert, and they started to swap letters discussing Albert's work.

Planck also sent his research assistant, Max Laue, to Bern to learn more about Albert and his theories. Max didn't realize that Albert had an ordinary job as a patent clerk. He thought he'd find Einstein working at the university. When Max first met Albert, he could scarcely believe that such a young man could be the "father of relativity." He joined Albert on a long walk around Bern. In the two hours that they chatted, Albert astonished Max by overthrowing a stack of long-accepted scientific ideas. Excited, Max described Albert to a colleague as a scientific revolutionary.

Another scientist who had spotted the importance of special relativity was Hermann Minkowski. He was Albert's former math professor from the Zurich Polytechnic! Minkowski was surprised to find that his laziest student, Albert Einstein, was the author of such an incredible piece of work. "I really would not have believed him capable of it," he later admitted. As a mathematician, Hermann saw how special relativity could be understood geometrically. He proposed adding a fourth dimension to the three dimensions of space—the dimension of time. It is this interweaving of space and time that creates the fabric of the universe—what he called space-time. Albert didn't grasp the idea at first, but later it helped him piece together his theory of general relativity.

⋛ HIS HAPPIEST THOUGHT ⋛

In 1907, Albert was still worrying about special relativity. His theory showed that time and space are relative, but it only dealt with the special case of objects traveling at a steady speed in nice straight lines. Albert now wanted to rework special relativity so that it could explain the real universe, where things are speeding up and slowing down all the time. Albert knew he'd have to include an explanation of gravity if he was to produce a theory of general relativity. Gravity had been traditionally understood as the force of attraction that makes things fall to the ground and that keeps the planets in orbit around the sun. Albert's hero, Isaac Newton, had described it as an invisible force—just like magnetism, the invisible force that had fascinated Albert as a child. But even Newton had been unable to explain *what* gravity actually was. In any case, Albert knew that invisible forces needed to be thought about very carefully. For centuries, people had believed in the invisible ether, too. Then Albert's very own special relativity explained why experiments to find the ether had never worked—it didn't exist!

Newton had defined gravity as a force of attraction between objects. Newton's laws of gravitation describe how the more mass objects have and the closer they are, the stronger the force of gravity is between them. Every schoolchild learned Newton's laws by heart. Now Albert tried to forget these laws for a moment. He asked himself the simplest of questions: How could you know that gravity is a force? Albert was staring out the window of his office on the third floor when he had the "happiest thought." Albert wondered how it would feel to fall from the roof of the building opposite. Suddenly, he realized something obvious but overlooked—a falling person feels weightless. Weight is an effect caused by gravity. While accelerating toward the ground, a falling person doesn't feel the effects of gravity! That meant gravity and acceleration cancel each other out, so could they be the same? Was gravity the same as acceleration? This thought experiment led Albert toward a new theory of gravitation— and a step closer to a theory of general relativity.

⋛ ON THE MOVE ⋚

Now that his theories were starting to be taken seriously, Albert decided to look for work at a university. That way he could keep up to speed with the latest research. Albert began by squeezing in some part-time teaching at the University of Bern along with his day job. It wasn't a great success. Only three students showed up for his first class—all three were friends of Albert's!

Then, in October 1909, at the age of thirty, Albert got his first full-time academic position—extraordinary professor of theoretical physics at the University of Zurich. Albert was sad to leave the patent office, but his scientific career was beginning to take off, and he knew it was time to go.

Albert and Mileva moved to Zurich, where their second son, Eduard, was born in July 1910. It was a busy but happy time for them. They were glad to be back in the beautiful city where they had first met. However, it wasn't long before they were on the move again. Next, the German University in Prague offered Albert an even better job. The scruffy and disorganized young professor who had dreamed up special relativity was now in demand.

Albert's new job was a step up and paid better, but the move to Prague was a disaster. The locals weren't very friendly to Germans or to Jews. Albert and Mileva didn't fit in and never really felt at home there. Albert was luckier than Mileva—at least he found some friends among the community at the university. He also regularly got the chance to escape from Prague, traveling abroad to give lectures. Meanwhile, poor Mileva was stuck in their cramped apartment, looking after two young boys. It was a lonely and unhappy time for her.

Mileva was relieved when Albert got the chance of an even better job back at the Zurich Polytechnic. They packed up their things and returned to Switzerland. Throughout all these changes of address, Albert had been steadily working on the problem of gravitation, but the math was proving tricky. He still couldn't make the breakthrough he was hoping for. He needed some expert help. On top of that, he had another problem. A lot had changed since Mileva and Albert first met. They had shared many happy times and also many challenges together, but now, sadly, they were growing apart.

In 1914, Max Planck persuaded Albert to move to Berlin to take up a specially created professorship at the University of Berlin. It was a great honor, and Albert accepted the job. However, Mileva didn't want to move yet again. She gave Berlin a try, but it didn't turn out well. Mileva separated from Albert, taking their two sons, Hans and Eduard, back to Zurich with her. Albert broke down and cried when he waved goodbye to them at the train station. He felt very sad and coped by throwing himself back into his work.

World War I

By 1914, Germany, under the leadership of Kaiser Wilhelm II, had grown in power and military might. Other European nations, including Britain and France, had built up their armies and navies, too. The balance of power rested in two major military alliances one between Germany, Austria, and Italy, the other between France, Britain, and Russia. But the stability of these alliances and of peace in Europe was fragile. When the Austrian archduke Franz Ferdinand was murdered in June 1914, it drew Europe into what would become World War I—one of the most devastating wars in history. The United States declared war on Germany on April 6, 1917, and started sending troops to Europe to fight. World War I lasted from 1914 until 1918, and millions of people died.

SPEAKING UP FOR PEACE

Albert had arrived in Berlin at a turning point in world history. Europe stood on the brink of war. In the autumn of 1914, the murder of Austria's archduke Franz Ferdinand set off a chain reaction across Europe. Austria-Hungary declared war on Serbia. Shortly afterward, Germany went on the attack, declaring war on Russia and France and invading neutral Belgium. It was a nightmare for peace-loving Albert.

Albert didn't believe that war was the way to resolve conflict. He had been a pacifist since his youth. One of the reasons he had left Germany was to avoid military service. Now everywhere Albert went in Berlin, he saw soldiers.

Many of the people that Albert worked with at the university supported Germany's role in the conflict. Max Planck was just one of his friends who had signed a declaration justifying Germany's actions. Albert was disappointed. How could intelligent, scientific minds believe there was ever a just cause for war? Albert reacted by doing the opposite and signed a public letter against the war, calling for Europe to unite and put an end to the conflict. But only three other people signed it.

CHAPTER 6

SCIENCE SUPERSTAR

While Mileva and their sons went to live in Switzerland, Albert stayed in Germany. He had grown close with his cousin Elsa, who also lived in Berlin. Elsa was slightly older than Albert; she was divorced and had two grown-up daughters. After Albert separated from Mileva, he and Elsa became romantically involved, which was unusual for first cousins, but not unheard of. Albert and Elsa would spend the duration of the war in Berlin together.

At first the war appeared to be going well for Germany, and it looked like it might end quickly. But where the armies of both sides clashed in Western Europe, neither side could get the better of the other. The soldiers dug trenches in the ground along what was called the Western Front and fought with shells and machine guns to push their territories farther. This became known as trench warfare. For years, neither side advanced far, and both armies suffered heavy casualties.

The effects of this long-drawn-out conflict were felt back in Berlin by Albert and Elsa. Enemy warships blockaded German ports, preventing supply vessels from bringing in food and fuel. This resulted in food shortages. By 1917, there were soup kitchens and long lines for bread in the streets of Berlin.

During World War I, new weapons based on the latest science and technology were introduced. One of Albert's friends, the scientist Fritz Haber, created a terrifying new weapon for the German army—poison gas. Haber had previously invented a way to make fertilizer that helped feed the world, but now he had produced a deadly weapon of mass destruction. Haber's poison gas killed thousands in the trenches on the Western Front. Albert was depressed to see how technology had become a force for violence. He was appalled by the war and retreated into his study.

"I quietly pursue my peaceful studies and thoughts and only feel pity and disgust." —Albert Einstein

THE RACE FOR RELATIVITY

Albert's work continued. His new theory of gravity was starting to make sense, but he was still wrestling with the equations. It was exhausting work, but Albert refused to give up. He redoubled his efforts, skipping meals and working tirelessly. In the fall of 1915, one year into the war, it suddenly became more urgent that Albert finish his theory. There was now a danger that someone else might beat him to solving the problem of general relativity first!

A German mathematician named David Hilbert had attended one of Albert's lectures. Hilbert listened very carefully, and when Albert discussed where he had gotten stuck with the equations, Hilbert's eyes lit up. He was sure that he could work out the math! When Albert got wind of this, he was worried his rival would solve the equations for general relativity before he could. Albert was due to give a lecture at the Prussian Academy toward the end of the year. It was his big chance to publicly show that he had succeeded first. But could he finish his equations for relativity in time? The pressure was on.

≡ EXPLAINING GRAVITY ≡

Isaac Newton had worked out mathematical laws to predict how gravity would affect things. But Newton couldn't explain how matter created this invisible force. In November 1915, Albert finally made a breakthrough that could explain gravity. He tested out his new equation on an old problem—the strange orbit of Mercury. Astronomers had long been puzzled by Mercury as each time it went around the sun, its orbit changed slightly. This blip didn't fit with Newton's gravitational laws. But Albert was overjoyed to find that his new theory of gravity predicted Mercury's orbit perfectly. He'd done it!

Albert triumphantly presented his equations for gravity and general relativity to the Prussian Academy on November 25, 1915. Albert summed up the whole universe in an equation. It was an incredible achievement. His rival David Hilbert accepted defeat.

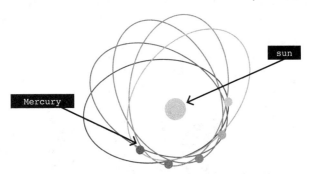

Albert's new theory of general relativity explained how gravity worked. It wasn't an invisible force that stretched instantly across space to pull things together. Instead, Albert theorized, gravity is the effect of mass warping the fabric of space-time. It is the curving of space-time that determines how objects move and interact. The mass of the sun warps the space-time around it, a bit like a heavy bowling ball warps the surface of a trampoline. If you roll a marble across a trampoline with a bowling ball on it, the marble appears to be attracted to the bowling ball, but it's really just following a path shaped by the warped trampoline. In the sun's case, not marbles but planets are deflected by warped space-time. It creates the orbits that the planets follow. Gravity is the result of the flexible, four-dimensional shape of space-time.

According to Albert's theory, it isn't just the paths of planets that can be deflected by the sun's gravitational field. The curving of space-time also affects how light travels. It can bend light! This realization gave Albert an idea for how to prove that general relativity is true. All he needed was a solar eclipse. But the war made it impossible to send expeditions around the world to observe one. Albert would have to wait for his proof.

Special vs. General

Special Theory of Relativity	General Theory of Relativity
For a special case	For general real-world situations
Just for objects moving in straight lines to or from each other	Applies to objects moving all over the place
Only for objects traveling at a constant speed	Works for objects speeding up, slowing down, and starting and stopping, too
Gravity not included	Gravity a key part of the package

Bending Light

Albert came up with a clever way to prove general relativity with a thought experiment. Albert imagined traveling in an elevator that had a small hole in one side with a light being shone through it.

If the elevator wasn't moving, the beam of light would shine straight onto the wall opposite. But if the elevator was accelerating upward, the light beam would appear to be bent downward. Albert had already shown that acceleration and gravity were indistinguishable, so gravity should have the same bending effect on light. If general relativity was true, astronomers would be able to observe the sun bending the path of distant starlight.

⋛ WANTED: SOLAR ECLIPSE ⋚

When Albert published his theory of general relativity in 1916, he proposed three tests to prove it. One of the tests predicted that the mass of the sun would bend light rays passing close to it—an effect that is now known as gravitational lensing. It means that the positions of stars as seen from Earth shift when the sun moves close by. Measuring the stars at night when there was no sun was easy. But measuring the position of stars close to the sun during the day was another matter. The sun was too bright! Both measurements were needed to show the shift in position caused by starlight bending through the warped space-time around the sun.

But Albert realized there was a perfect opportunity to get the measurements he needed: a total eclipse of the sun. When the moon's shadow blocks out the sun's rays, stars close to the sun can be photographed in the short period of darkness. Before he had even published his theory on general relativity, Albert had issued a challenge to astronomers to do just that. The German astronomer Erwin Freundlich had met Albert in Berlin and agreed to photograph the solar eclipse in Russia in 1914— but while he was there, war between Russia and Germany was declared. The Russian military confiscated Freundlich's equipment and he was briefly held prisoner! It would be several more years before Albert could take advantage of another solar eclipse.

⋚ OVERWORKED ALBERT ⋚

General relativity had taken Albert nearly a decade of intense work. The years from 1915 to 1917 were particularly hard on Albert's health as he put all of his energies into finishing his theory. Despite Elsa's care, Albert neglected himself during the most intense bursts of work. He smoked cigars and didn't eat properly. Albert got sick with bad stomach pains and suddenly lost a lot of weight. His doctor gave him a checkup and soon found the cause—Albert had developed a stomach ulcer. He was told to rest, and the doctor put him on a simple diet to help his stomach recover. Elsa moved him into her apartment to nurse him back to health.

The shortages of food and fuel in Berlin made life particularly hard in the winter of 1917. The weather was bitterly cold. Albert took to his bed—it was the only warm place in the apartment! Things had gotten so bad in Berlin that Albert's mother, who had moved back to the south of Germany, had to send Albert food parcels.

RACE TO THE SUN

The war made it difficult for German scientists to communicate with other scientists around the world. But a translation of Albert's work on general relativity found its way into the hands of the British astronomer Arthur Eddington. He admired it and became a strong supporter of Albert's theory. He shared Einstein's paper on relativity with Britain's top astronomer, the astronomer royal, Sir Frank Dyson. He was also impressed.

Arthur was a conscientious objector—he refused to fight during the war because he was against violence and killing. He felt a close sympathy with Albert as a fellow pacifist. Arthur thought that the scientific community could help heal the divisions created by the war. By working together with Albert Einstein, Germany's leading scientist, Arthur hoped to set an example of international cooperation.

There was no time to lose. The race was on, with astronomers around the world competing to be the first to prove or disprove relativity. On May 29, 1919, there was going to be a solar eclipse. Who would get to it first? Sir Frank Dyson organized two expeditions. They would photograph the position of the stars during the six minutes and fifty-one seconds of the eclipse. Arthur Eddington led one expedition and sailed to Príncipe, an island off the west coast of Africa. The second expedition traveled to Sobral, in Brazil. Meanwhile, Albert waited in Berlin for news.

Eclipse of the Sun

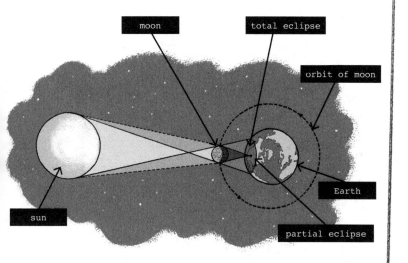

Never look directly at an eclipse! Even just a few seconds of exposure can cause permanent damage to your eyes. Scientists and astronomers use specialized equipment to observe this natural phenomenon. If you have the opportunity to view an eclipse, make sure you wear a special set of eclipse glasses. These should be less than three years old, and the manufacturer's name and address should appear somewhere on the glasses. Normal sunglasses won't protect you!

Warp Factor

General relativity predicted that light rays traveling close to the sun would bend. The sun is a huge ball of fiery gases. It contains a lot of matter and so has a lot of mass. Albert predicted that the gravitational effect of the sun's mass would distort space-time. Light traveling through this gravitational field would bend to follow the curving of space-time. Measurements could show whether there was any difference between each star's apparent and true position. Any shift would be direct evidence that light had bent and that space-time was warped.

RELATIVITY WINS!

On November 6, 1919, a special joint meeting of the Royal Astronomical Society and the Royal Society was held in London. Scientists and reporters packed the hall. Everyone knew they were about to witness a great event in scientific history. Finally the world would discover if Albert Einstein's theory of general relativity was correct. Would this unknown German professor overturn the ideas of Isaac Newton?

A hush came over the crowded hall as Sir Frank Dyson spoke:

> "After careful study of the photos, I am prepared to say that there can be no doubt that they confirm Einstein's predictions."

The positions of the stars *had* shifted slightly—Albert was right! It was a historic moment. The press ran with the science story of the century. A few doubters surfaced after the meeting. They pointed out issues with Eddington's data, but later eclipse expeditions reconfirmed Einstein's theory.

Albert had already been tipped off in a telegram from a friend, the Dutch physicist Hendrik Lorentz. Hendrik had told him that even though the results were a little shaky, the expedition had been a success. What Albert didn't know was just how massive an impact relativity was about to make on the world.

The following day, the front page of the *Times* newspaper of London led with the triumph of Einstein's relativity. The story made it clear to the general public that Albert Einstein, a former patent clerk turned professor, had totally changed the

NOVEMBER 10, 1919

LIGHTS ALL ASKEW IN THE HEAVENS

way we look at the universe. In the United States, the *New York Times* led with a headline inspired by how gravity had bent the path of starlight.

Relativity touched a chord with everyone, as did the scruffy, forty-year-old professor with the wild hair. He was already everyone's idea of what a genius should look like. Albert had wanted his work to be recognized, not himself! But he was about to get a whole lot more attention than he had bargained for. Albert Einstein was now a science superstar!

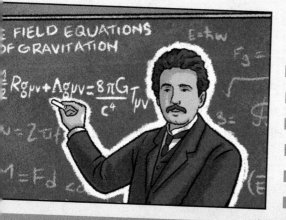

⋛ ENDING AND BEGINNING ⋚

The same year that Albert made front-page news with relativity also saw big changes in his personal life. In February 1919, Albert and Mileva were divorced. To ensure that Mileva had enough money to care for the boys, Albert offered her the money that came with the Nobel Prize. The only thing was, he hadn't won it yet! But Mileva accepted his offer—she believed in Albert's genius and was sure he would win sooner or later. Four months after the divorce, Albert married Elsa.

Meanwhile, the news about Einstein and relativity spread like wildfire around the world. People were curious about this amazing new theory and wanted to understand what all the excitement was about. Newspapers and magazines were filled with articles in which experts tried to explain Albert's theories. At first being a celebrity was fun, but Albert soon discovered the downside of fame. He needed peace and quiet to think and work, but now he was constantly interrupted. An endless stream of journalists phoned or visited the apartment. It seemed like everyone wanted something from Albert. He was overwhelmed with requests to give an interview or a quote, or to present a talk or lecture.

The craze for relativity meant that Albert was always in the public eye. Everything he said was reported and ended up in print. Not all the stories were positive—some even poked fun at Albert and relativity. Albert compared himself to King Midas, the mythical king who turned all he touched to gold. Except, he added, everything *he* touched turned into newsprint!

Elsa worked hard to protect her husband from the pressures of fame. She took his calls, dealt with the sackfuls of invitations and letters he received, and generally tried to keep visitors from disturbing him.

CHAPTER 7
AFTER RELATIVITY

Germany's defeat in World War I had left the country in a terrible state. There were shortages of food and fuel, and German money lost its value, so everything became very expensive. Many people were hungry, unemployed, and struggling to survive. Germans looked for someone to blame for their problems. Jewish people became the main target of their anger.

A movement called the National Socialist German Workers' Party (Nazi Party) used these anti-Jewish feelings to help its quest for power. Scientists who supported the Nazis started a campaign against Albert because he was a famous Jewish scientist. The German physicist Philipp Lenard, who had won a Nobel Prize in 1905, joined the campaign. He criticized Albert and spoke scornfully about his theory of relativity during a big public meeting. Berlin was becoming dangerous for Albert. Elsa worried for Albert's safety and thought they should leave Germany.

Book Burnings

Later, in spring 1933, the Nazis staged public book burnings, where literature they considered to be un-German was destroyed. Albert's book on general relativity was one the books that the Nazis threw into the flames.

The Nazi Party

Among the defeated soldiers returning from the trenches after World War I was a 29-year-old army corporal named Adolf Hitler. He joined the Nazi Party and soon became its leader. Hitler was a powerful speaker, and his confidence inspired lots of desperate people. The Nazi Party rapidly grew until it controlled Germany. Hitler wrote a book about his life and his extremist views titled *Mein Kampf* (which means "My Struggle" in German). In the book, he falsely blames the Jews for Germany's problems and says they are a threat to its future. His hate-filled ideas led the Nazis to systematically murder six million Jews—and kill millions of others targeted for political, social, or racial reasons—before World War II ended in 1945.

⋛ WORLD TOUR ⋚

Albert agreed it was time to take a break from Germany. In 1920, he set off on a world tour with Elsa by his side. The whirlwind adventure took them to Hong Kong, Singapore, China, Japan, Palestine, and Spain. Einstein met many important people along the way, including a Japanese empress at a garden party and the king of Spain!

Albert gave fascinating lectures in every country, sharing his scientific ideas with thousands of people. Journalists and huge crowds turned out to listen to Albert wherever he went. But Albert also used his fame to speak up against the Nazis, and he tried to warn the world about the danger of another war. He played the violin at charity concerts and even sold photos of himself to raise money to help poor people back in Germany.

⋛ MEETING AND GREETING ⋛

One of the first countries that Albert and Elsa visited was the United States. They sailed on a passenger liner to New York in the spring of 1921. A crowd of twenty thousand waited to greet them as they stepped off the ship. They traveled to city hall with the mayor of New York in a procession of open-topped cars. Albert stood in the back of his car and waved to the cheering crowds.

During his two-month tour of America, Albert got a warm welcome almost everywhere he went. However, when Albert reached Washington, DC, the president of the United States refused to meet him! President Warren Harding mistakenly thought that Albert was one of the scientists who signed the letter supporting Germany's actions at the start of World War I. Once the president realized his mistake, he welcomed Albert and Elsa to the White House, and they had a photograph taken with him on the lawn.

NOBEL PRIZE WINNER

While they were traveling around East Asia in 1922, Albert got a message saying that he had finally won the Nobel Prize for Physics! After a decade of nominations and disappointments, Albert was thrilled to have won. But he was surprised that it was for his earlier work on the photoelectric effect, not for his theory of general relativity! Albert ignored this detail when he gave his acceptance speech in Sweden the following year. He spoke about general relativity and went on to preview his next work, a "unified theory" that covered gravity and electricity—basically a theory of everything!

Winning the Nobel Prize also meant that Albert could finally honor the divorce deal he had made with Mileva. He gave her the prize money so that his two sons would be financially secure for the future.

DANGEROUS DAYS

The situation for Jews in Germany worsened year by year. In June 1922, the German foreign minister, Walther Rathenau, a prominent Jew, was murdered by three members of an anti-Semitic terrorist group. Albert had been a friend of Walther Rathenau and was appalled by his brutal murder. He also started to worry that, as a high-profile Jew, he might be targeted next. He had kept his permanent residence in Berlin, thinking that extremists like Hitler and the Nazi Party would soon fail in their quest for power. But he was being proved wrong.

QUANTUM QUARREL

Meanwhile, Albert's scientific work continued. He was now in his forties and no longer the young rebel scientist. He continued to work on his new theory, but his best ideas were probably behind him. A new generation of scientists was following in his footsteps, including a Danish physicist named Niels Bohr and Niels's former assistant, German physicist Werner Heisenberg.

NIELS BOHR

A young Albert had blazed a trail with his theories of packets of light and energy called quanta. Inspired by Albert's work, Niels and Werner developed quantum theory further. Their ideas were groundbreaking, but too radical for Albert. They argued that chance, like a roll of a dice, was behind many events in the universe. Albert believed the universe followed stricter laws.

Though I am now an old fogey, I am still hard at work and still refuse to believe that God plays dice.

Following their first meeting in Berlin in 1920, Albert and Niels continued their good-natured quantum quarrel for years. Niels admired Albert and was sad that he couldn't persuade his hero to accept the new theory. But Albert's counterarguments and challenges made a positive contribution to quantum science. They helped shape a branch of science that made technology such as computers possible. Quantum theory continues to be an exciting field of research today.

TIME TO REST

As the 1920s progressed, Albert's health took a turn for the worse. In 1928, he collapsed while on a trip to Switzerland. Albert's doctors told him that his heart was enlarged and that he should take it easy from now on. Albert hired Helen Dukas as a personal assistant to help with his workload. She knew nothing about science but was a great organizer. Albert spent a couple of months recovering in the countryside along with Elsa in their summer house in Caputh, in northeast Germany. The house was close to the water, so Albert could relax by sailing on the lakes. Albert and Elsa visited Caputh whenever they could, but they knew the peace they found there couldn't last.

⋛ A LUCKY ESCAPE ⋚

In January 1933, Hitler was named chancellor of Germany, and the rise of the Nazis became unstoppable. Albert was on his way to teach in America when he heard the terrible news. He knew that soon he would have to leave Germany. When they had left their summer house in December, Albert had advised Elsa to take a last look, telling her they would never see it again.

Just months later, Nazi soldiers broke into the same house and turned it upside down, searching for evidence to discredit Albert. They found nothing, but Albert was still branded an enemy of the German state. His property and money were seized by the Nazis, and a reward was offered for Albert's capture. The Nazis printed a list of their enemies, and Albert was on it. Under his photograph was the chilling caption "not hanged yet."

Over the next few years, the Nazis introduced a series of terrifying laws and restrictions that limited what Jews could do:

1933 • Jews are no longer allowed to work in the government or as lawyers.

1935 • Jewish soldiers are dismissed from the German army.
• Jewish people lose their right to German citizenship.

1936 • Jewish teachers are not allowed to work in public schools.

1938 • Jewish people must report all property worth over 5,000 Reichsmarks. The Nazis transferred much of this property to non-Jewish Germans.
• Jewish people must have the letter *J* stamped on their passports.
• All Jewish-owned businesses are forced to close.

Albert knew that Nazi scientists such as Philipp Lenard would put pressure on the Prussian Academy of Sciences to expel him, so he denied them the chance to do that and resigned. Shortly afterward, Hitler ordered that Jewish academics be forced out of their jobs in German universities. Albert had been lucky to escape just in time—but he was worried about the other Jewish scientists who were still stuck there!

While in Britain, Albert met with Winston Churchill, an influential member of Parliament, who would later become prime minister. Albert asked Churchill to do what he could to help Jewish scientists get out of Germany before it was too late.

THE REFUGEE PROFESSOR

In 1932, Albert had been offered a job at a new research facility at Princeton University. Here, he would be free to work without distraction. Albert and Elsa arrived in America in October 1933. They had brought Albert's personal assistant, Helen Dukas, with them. It was a low-key arrival compared to their first trip to the United States. This time the ocean liner that sailed into New York carried hundreds of

German Jews who were fleeing the horrors of Nazi Germany, just like the Einsteins.

Albert and Elsa loved Princeton. It was green and peaceful, like a country village. After all the worry of life in Germany, they felt safe at last. They rented a big house and had a housewarming party. Albert entertained his guests by playing a few tunes on his violin, of course.

At fifty-four years old, Albert was not in the best of health. From now on, he rarely ventured far from Princeton. All he really wanted to do was quietly work on the unified field theory. Albert asked for an office with the bare basics, including a large wastepaper bin for all his mistakes. Then he got down to work. Every day he'd walk to his office, wearing his trademark scruffy clothes and no socks. Sometimes he would ride his bicycle. In his spare time, he still played music or sailed his little boat to relax. It was a quiet life, but it suited him.

Life is like riding a bicycle. To keep your balance, you must keep moving.

A SAD FAREWELL

In 1935, Albert and Elsa bought their own home in Princeton. It was a large house, and Albert's study had a window that overlooked a lovely garden. They were excited about living there together, but then Elsa became sick with heart and kidney disease—it was serious. By the winter of 1936, Elsa was forced to stay in bed. Albert sat beside his wife, reading and chatting to her whenever he could. Elsa died just before Christmas that year. Albert was heartbroken. He plunged ever deeper into his work on unified field theory to distract himself.

ATOMIC ANXIETIES

In August 1939, Albert was relaxing at his summer house in Long Island when two visitors paid a surprise call. They were both Hungarian physicists. Leo Szilard and Eugene Wigner needed Albert's help. Back in 1905, Albert had shown in his equation $E = mc^2$ that, theoretically, it was possible to release a vast amount of energy from a tiny atom. Leo had worked out a way to do just that using a chain reaction. He'd also figured out that the energy released could be used in a devastating new weapon—the atom bomb. Leo was worried that the Germans were already working on this and might get the bomb first!

Leo and Eugene told Albert about this threat.

They persuaded him to sign a letter advising US president Franklin Roosevelt to start developing a nuclear bomb before the Germans. Albert was still a pacifist, but he feared a world run by the Nazis. He signed the letter. This decision worried Albert for the rest of his life. When atomic bombs were dropped on Japan at the end of World War II, Albert was horrified. He went on to become one of the world's most outspoken campaigners against nuclear weapons.

WORKING TO THE LAST

Albert retreated to his study and to his equations more and more as he drew to the end of his life. After World War II, Albert officially retired from the Institute for Advanced Study, but he still went to his office and pondered the equations of the unified field theory that eluded him to the end of his days.

Albert was tired and ill in his later years, but his mind remained sharp. He carried on campaigning for world peace right to the end of his life. Then, in April 1955, Albert suffered an enlargement of the main artery from his heart. The doctors told him he needed surgery, but Albert refused it. He said it was "tasteless" to prolong life artificially and that he was ready to go. The pain was bad, but he asked for paper and a pencil. Even in his hospital bed, he worked to the last, covering page after page with equations. On Monday, April 18, 1955, at the age of seventy-six, Albert died in Princeton Hospital.

CONCLUSION

CHANGING THE WORLD

Albert Einstein changed the way we see the universe. The equations of general relativity have become part of the basic tool kit for astrophysicists and scientists. They are used in practical everyday ways, such as fine-tuning the measurements of navigation satellites. Thanks to general relativity, we can accurately see where we are on a smartphone map! Radio telescopes and space telescopes have shown us the effects of curved space-time that Albert imagined more than a hundred years ago.

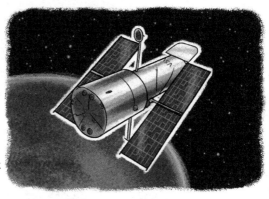

Albert's work laid the foundations for all kinds of science that continue today. Astronomers and theoretical physicists have gone on to use general relativity to unlock some of the secrets of our universe. Before relativity, most scientists had thought the universe was unmoving, but Einstein's equations suggested that it was expanding. Even Albert thought this could not be right. He corrected his math, adding something called a "cosmological constant" to cancel out this expansion. Then in 1929, the US astronomer Edwin Hubble showed that the universe really *was* expanding.

Hubble worked at the Mount Wilson Observatory in Los Angeles, which at that time had the world's largest telescope. He used this to observe distant stars. Hubble figured out that a shift in the color of light from faraway galaxies showed that they were all moving apart, just as Albert's original general relativity equations had predicted! Albert hadn't needed to add that special cosmological constant. When Albert found out, he told everyone that he had made a big blunder! Albert considered mistakes part of the thinking process and once said that:

> Anyone who has never made a mistake has never tried anything new.

⋛ THE BIG BANG ⋚

There was another important discovery that resulted from Hubble's discovery. An expanding universe led astronomers to wonder about how it had all begun. They used their measurements and general relativity to work backward, "rewinding" the universe to when it began. This led to a theory known as the big bang. The idea is that all the matter and energy in the universe started out from a super-hot, super-dense point known as a singularity. This suddenly expanded 13.8 billion years ago, cooling as it spread out to form stars, galaxies, and planets.

There's a strange twist to the story of Albert's cosmological constant—it made a comeback. Theoretically, gravity should slow down the expansion of the universe, but just over fifty years ago, scientists discovered it was doing exactly the opposite. The galaxies farthest away were actually speeding up as they raced away from us. Scientists now think it is the influence of a mysterious and invisible type of matter called dark matter that cancels out the effects of gravity to speed up this expansion of the universe. Einstein's cosmological constant has been brought back into play for the math that describes this effect. Maybe his big blunder explains the universe after all!

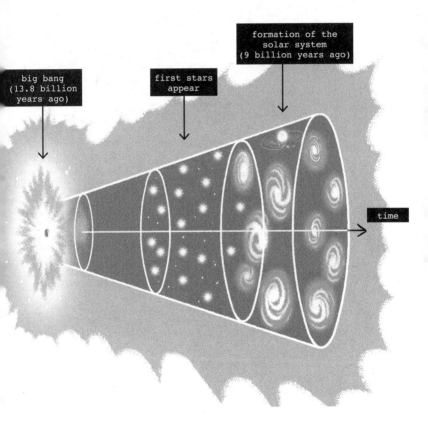

BLACK HOLES

Solving the equations of general relativity also predicted strange astronomical objects called black holes. Black holes are regions of space-time where gravity is so strong that nothing can escape from them, not even light. They are areas of super-dense matter thought to form when some types of stars collapse in on themselves. Albert was skeptical that they really existed, but his theory showed they were possible. Scientists such as the astrophysicist Stephen Hawking also did pioneering work on black holes using general relativity. On April 10, 2019, scientists using an array of radio telescopes from around the world captured the first-ever image of a black hole. This was the first visual evidence that black holes existed.

The flexible fabric of space-time described by general relativity also led Albert to predict that waves of gravity could travel through the universe. Gravitational waves are set off by the acceleration of large masses. These energy waves then travel through the universe at the speed of light. Albert's prediction of gravitational waves was proved true in 2016, when scientists detected the ripples in space-time caused by two black holes merging.

⋛ STRANGE BUT TRUE ⋚

Albert's equations for general relativity work well for large objects like planets, stars, and galaxies. However, the math starts to break down when it comes to the small-scale universe and dealing with the behavior of atoms and the tiniest particles they are made from. Einstein had laid the groundwork for quantum mechanics, which went on to describe the universe at this small scale. Quantum mechanics led to new technology such as lasers, transistors, and computers. It is being used today to develop new, super-powerful quantum computers.

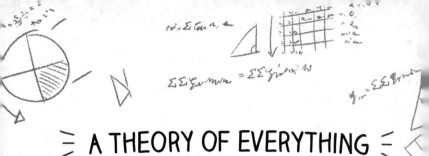

A THEORY OF EVERYTHING

Albert spent the latter years of his career in America working on his unified field theory, what he called a theory of everything. Right to the end, when he was dying in the hospital, he was scribbling on a piece of paper, working on equations that might bring unity to these different theories. He didn't succeed, but scientists are still very interested in unified field theory. Maybe another curious mind will imagine a solution to the problem Albert didn't manage to solve!

Albert also spent much of his life trying to bring unity to the world. He had lived through two world wars, and toward the end of his life he was working on a public document to promote world peace. In a time when nuclear weapons could destroy the earth, it was more important than ever that governments made a commitment to peace. Albert may not have seen his dream of truly united nations living together in peace, but his vision has continued to inspire others to work for the same ideals.

We invite this Congress, and through it the scientists of the world and the general public, to subscribe to the following resolution:

"In view of the fact that in any future world war nuclear weapons will certainly be employed, and that such weapons threaten the continued existence of mankind, we urge the governments of the world to realize, and to acknowledge publicly, that their purpose cannot be furthered by a world war, and we urge them, consequently, to find peaceful means for the settlement of all matters of dispute between them."

A MODEST GENIUS

Albert was never happy with the idea of being revered as a genius. He wouldn't have wanted anyone to give up on themselves because they hadn't been born with brilliant intelligence. Albert always claimed that he had no special talents other than curiosity and the ability to stick with a problem, no matter how tough it seemed.

When his son Eduard was nine years old, Eduard asked his father why he was famous. Albert told Eduard that the only difference between himself and a blind beetle crawling around a curved branch was that he was lucky enough to have noticed that the branch was curved. It was a modest and funny answer, but it contained a serious truth—to discover something new, you might need to look at things from a completely different angle. Albert did exactly that, and thanks to him, we can see our universe differently, too.

Timeline

March 14
Albert Einstein is born in Ulm, Germany.

October
Albert Einstein starts training to be a teacher Zurich Polytech and meets Mile Marić.

1879

1896

Thomas Edison patents the first commercial light bulb.

January 28
A pacifist, Albert Einstein gives up German citizenship to avoid military service.

July 28
Eduard Einstein is born.

1905

1910

Albert Einstein publishes five significant science articles, including one on what will become known as special relativity, and a follow-up article containing the equation $E = mc^2$.

1902 — 1903 — 1904

June 23
Albert Einstein starts work at the Swiss patent office in Bern.

May 14
Hans Einstein is born.

Lieserl Einstein is born.

January 6
Albert Einstein marries Mileva Marić.

1914 — 1918 — 1919

November 11
World War I ends.

Albert Einstein divorces his first wife, Mileva Marić, and marries his cousin Elsa.

July 28
World War I begins.

November 6
It is publicly announced in London that the solar eclipse confirms that general relativity is correct.

April 2
Albert Einstein starts a world tour, visits the United States, and raises funds for the Hebrew University in Jerusalem.

November 9
Albert Einstein wins Nobel Prize Physics for his on light and t photoelectric eff not relativity

1921   1922

June 24
Walther Rathenau, German foreign minist and friend of Albert Einstein, is murdered

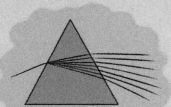

Albert Einstein becomes a US citizen.

1939   1940   1941

September 1
World War II begins in Europe.

December 7
Japan makes a surprise attac on Pearl Harbor Hawaii. The Uni States joins World War II.

1929 1933 1936

January 30
Adolf Hitler becomes chancellor of Germany. Albert and Elsa Einstein emigrate to the United States, where he joins the faculty of the Institute for Advanced Study at Princeton, New Jersey.

October 24
The Great Depression begins in the United States.

December 20
Albert Einstein's second wife, Elsa, dies.

1945 1955

August 6
The first atomic bomb is dropped on Hiroshima, Japan. Another is dropped on Nagasaki on August 9.

April 18
Albert Einstein dies from a burst artery in Princeton Hospital at the age 76.

September 2
World War II ends.

Further Reading

→ *Awesome Physics Experiments for Kids* by Erica L. Colón, PhD (Rockridge Press, 2019)

→ *The Cartoon Guide to Physics* (Cartoon Guide Series) by Larry Gonick and Art Huffman (HarperPerennial, 1991)

→ *National Geographic Kids: Albert Einstein* by Libby Romero (National Geographic Children's Books, 2016)

→ *The Ultimate Quotable Einstein* edited by Alice Calaprice (Princeton University Press, 2011)

Websites

→ albert-einstein.org
A website including an extensive archive of Einstein's notes, along with games and photos.

→ history.aip.org/history/exhibits/einstein/index.html
A website with a timeline and photos spanning Albert Einstein's life.

Glossary

anti-Semitism: Hostility and racial discrimination against Jewish people.

atomic bomb: A bomb that gets its power from the rapid release of nuclear energy, causing huge amounts of damage.

bar mitzvah: A religious celebration of a Jewish boy's thirteenth birthday.

black hole: A region of space with such an intense gravitational field that no matter can escape.

cosmological: Relating to the universe.

ether: An invisible substance once thought to be the medium that light waves travel through.

Glossary

geometry: The branch of math concerned with shapes and their properties.

gravity: The attraction between two objects that have mass, making them move toward each other.

merchant: A person involved in trading goods.

pacifism: Opposition to violence and war and a belief in peaceful methods to sort out conflict.

patent: The proof of the ownership of an idea or invention for a period of time.

propaganda: A one-sided use of information to influence people's beliefs.

Glossary

quantum: A small packet of energy.

synagogue: A meeting place where Jews gather to worship or to learn more about their religion.

Western Front: The area of Western Europe where the opposing armies of World War I clashed and fought a long-drawn-out war from their trenches.

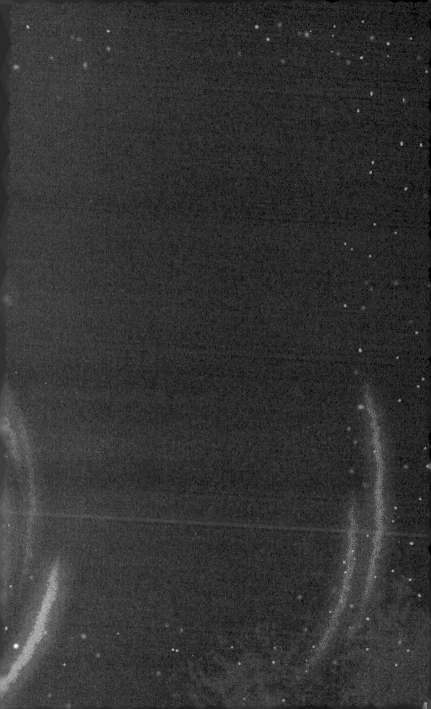

Index

A

Africa, 2, 6
   Príncipe, 110
algebra, 33
Annalen der Physik, 71, 74, 86
anti-Semitism, 27–29, 44, 91, 119, 121, 126, 158, 130–133
astronomers
   Dyson, Sir Frank, 109–110, 113
   Eddington, Arthur, 109–110
   Freundlich, Erwin, 106–107
astrophysicists, 139, 144
Atlantic Ocean, 2
atoms, 74, 135–137, 145, 155
Austria, 94–95
   Austria-Hungary, 95
   Salzburg, 37

B

Belgium, 95
Besso, Michele, 56, 67, 76–77
big bang theory, 142
black holes, 144
Bohr, Niels, 126–128

C

Churchill, Winston, 132

D

dark matter, 142
Dukas, Helen, 128, 132

E

eclipse, *see* solar eclipse
Edison, Thomas, 16, 152
Einstein, Eduard, 91, 93, 97, 116, 125, 148, 152
Einstein, Elsa, 97–98, 108, 116, 118–119, 122–124, 128, 130, 132–133, 135, 153, 155
Einstein, Hans Albert, 68, 93, 97, 116, 125, 153
Einstein, Hermann, 12, 14, 17, 19, 22, 44, 46, 51, 61, 63, 66, 85
Einstein, Jakob, 8, 14, 33, 44, 51
Einstein, Lieserl, 65, 153
Einstein, Maja, 19–20, 24, 42–44, 46, 82
Einstein, Pauline, 12, 15, 17, 19–20, 24, 26, 38, 46, 58, 66, 85, 109

Index

electricity, 16, 124
energy, 6, 72–74, 80–81, 127, 135–136, 141
equations, 3, 33, 80–81, 84, 100–101, 135, 138–141, 144–146, 152
ether, 51, 53, 72, 88, 158

F
Ferdinand, Franz, 94–95
France, 94–95

G
Galileo, Galilei, 4, 55
geometry, 33, 68
Germany, 16, 45, 51, 61, 94–97, 119, 121, 134, 128, 130, 132–133
   Berlin, 38, 93, 95, 97–98, 109–110, 119, 126, 128
   German empire, 30–31
   Munich, 14, 19, 41, 46–47, 50
   Ulm, 11, 14
gravity 5, 88–89, 92, 100–101, 103–106, 142, 144
Grossmann, Marcel, 56, 64

H
Haber, Fritz, 100
Haller, Friedrich, 64–65, 85
Hawking, Stephen, 144
Heisenberg, Werner, 126–127
Hilbert, David, 100–101
Hitler, Adolf, 121, 126, 130, 132, 155
Hubble, Edwin, 140–142

I
Italy, 44, 47, 50
   Milan, 46, 66

J
Japan, 137
Judaism, 12, 27, 34, 40, 158

L
Laue, Max, 86
light, 6, 9, 16, 51, 53, 55, 71–73, 76–77, 79–80, 103–106, 112, 127, 141, 144, 151, 153, 158

Index

M

magnetism, 23
Marić, Mileva, 58–62, 64–68, 91–93, 97, 116, 125, 152–153
Michelson, Albert, 53
military, 29–31, 47, 94–95, 107, 152
Minkowski, Hermann, 87
molecules, 74
Morley, Edward, 53
Mozart, Wolfgang Amadeus, 36–37
music, 24–26, 36–39, 122, 123

N

Nazis, 119–122, 126, 130–133, 137
Newton, Isaac, 5, 76, 88–89, 101, 113
Nobel Prize, 116, 119, 124–125
nuclear power, 81, 136–137, 146–147

O

Olympia Academy, 67, 71

P

pacifism, 30, 95–96, 110, 132, 137–138, 146–147
patent office, job at, 64–65, 67, 68–69, 83–85, 91
physics, theoretical, 57
Planck, Max, 2, 86, 93, 96
Prague, 91
Prussian Academy, 100–101

Q

quantum energy, 72–73, 126–128, 145

R

Rathenau, Walter, 126, 155
relativity, 4, 5, 6, 9, 55, 79–80, 86–89, 100–101, 104, 106, 110, 112–114, 116–117, 124, 139–141, 144
space-time, 79, 87, 103, 106, 112, 139, 144
unified theory of, 124, 134–135, 138, 146
Roosevelt, Franklin, 137
Russia, 94–95, 106–107, 139

Index

S

school, 7, 27–29, 31–33, 41–43, 46–49, 50–52, 54–56, 58, 60
   Aarau school, 54–56
   Luitpold Gymnasium, 29
   Zurich Polytechnic, 51–52, 56, 58, 62, 67, 87, 92, 152
   see also universities
Serbia, 95
solar eclipse, 2, 6, 9, 103, 106–107, 110–111
solar system, 103, 106, 112, 140–142, 144
South America, 2, 6
   Sobral, Brazil, 110
Swan, Joseph, 16
Switzerland, 51, 61, 92, 97, 128
   Bern 64, 66–68, 76
   patent office of, 64–65, 68–69, 83–85, 91
   Zurich, 91, 93
Szilard, Leo, 135–136

T

Talmud, Bernard, 48
Talmud, Max, 34–36, 42, 46, 47

time, 6, 76–77, 87, 103

U

United Kingdom, 9, 94, 132
   England, 2
   London, 113–114
United States, 9, 94, 115, 123, 132, 146
   Long Island, 135
   Los Angeles, 141
   New York, 46, 123, 132
   Princeton, 133–135, 138
   Washington, D.C., 124
universe, 3, 5, 8, 57, 78–79, 87–88, 101, 115, 127, 130, 140, 142–143, 145, 148
universities
   Hebrew University, 154
   Princeton University, 132
   University of Berlin, 93
   University of Bern, 90
   University of Prague, 91
   University of Zurich, 74–75, 91

Index

V

von Bismarck, Otto, 31

W

Wigner, Eugene, 135–136

Wilhelm, Ostad, 63

Wilhelm II, 30, 94

World War I, 3, 9, 94–99, 119, 121, 124

World War II, 121, 137–138

FOLLOW THE TRAIL!

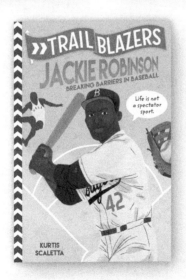

TURN THE PAGE FOR A SNEAK PEEK AT THESE TRAILBLAZERS BIOGRAPHIES!

Excerpt text copyright © 2020 by Ebony Joy Wilkins.
Excerpt illustrations copyright © 2020 by Rachel Sanson.
Cover art copyright © 2020 by Luisa Uribe. Published in the United
States by Random House Children's Books, a division of Penguin
Random House LLC, New York.

TRAIL BLAZERS
BEYONCÉ
QUEEN OF THE SPOTLIGHT

Power means hard work.

EBONY JOY WILKINS

WORKING HARD

One by one, the girls went up in front of Deborah and Denise to audition for a group called Girls Tyme. Beyoncé gave her performance everything she had, then waited to hear the verdict. Would it be enough? Finally, once everyone in the room had sung, Denise and Deborah read out a list of names.

"Beyoncé!" they called. "You're in." She had made it! One of the other successful girls was LaTavia Roberson, a young singer whom Denise and Deborah had worked with previously. The group began practicing right away. On several evenings each week, Mathew or Tina dropped Beyoncé off at Denise and Deborah's office. There, the girls learned techniques for strengthening their voices and creating harmonies. They began performing at small venues around Houston and auditioning for music showcases and TV commercials.

An investor named Andretta "Ann" Tillman watched one of their performances and thought that the group had serious potential. She offered financial backing but wanted to make a few changes to the lineup and to hire professional producer and songwriter Lonnie Jackson.

Over the next few months, Denise, Deborah, Andretta, and Lonnie cut some of the singers from Girls Tyme and brought others in. The group grew to include Kelendria "Kelly" Rowland, a talented singer and friend of LaTavia's who had recently moved to Texas from Georgia. Kelly's father had fought in the Vietnam War and struggled with post-traumatic stress disorder, a mental health condition usually triggered by a stressful event. The strain on the family had led Kelly's mother to move to Texas in search of a fresh start. Like Beyoncé, Kelly was an amazing singer, but shy. The two girls hit it off at once.

⋛ A NEW PARTNERSHIP ⋛

Jay-Z and Beyoncé released a single together, "'03 Bonnie and Clyde." On the track, Jay-Z sings, "All I need in this life of sin is me and my girlfriend," to which Beyoncé replies, "Down to ride till the very end, is me and my boyfriend." For some fans, this was confirmation enough that the two were dating.

But even with rumors swirling, Beyoncé and Jay-Z refused to confirm or deny that they were together. When asked about the nature of their relationship, Jay-Z told one reporter, "She's beautiful. Who wouldn't wish she was their girlfriend? Maybe one day."

Bonnie and Clyde

Jay-Z and Beyoncé's track was named after two infamous criminals who traveled the United States together in the 1930s. Bonnie and Clyde led police on a chase across the country, robbing several businesses and murdering 13 people. The two were finally tracked down by a Texas Ranger in Bienville Parish, Louisiana, where they were shot and killed.

Excerpt text copyright © 2019 by Alex Woolf.
Excerpt illustrations copyright © 2019 by Artful Doodlers.
Cover art copyright © 2019 by Luisa Uribe and George Ermos.
Published in the United States by Random House Children's Books,
a division of Penguin Random House LLC, New York.

TRAIL BLAZERS
NEIL ARMSTRONG
FIRST MAN ON THE MOON

One small step for man...

ALEX WOOLF

⋛ FLYING LESSONS ⋛

Airplanes remained Neil's first love. His dream was to become both a pilot and an aeronautical engineer—someone who designs and builds planes. About three or four miles outside Wapakoneta was Port Koneta Airport. Neil cycled or hitchhiked there as often as he could to watch the planes land and take off, and talk to the pilots.

When he was fifteen, Neil began saving up for flying lessons. He got a job at Rhine and Brading's Pharmacy, where he earned forty cents an hour. A one-hour flying lesson cost nine dollars, so he had to work twenty-two and a half hours to pay for one lesson! Neil supplemented his earnings at the pharmacy by offering to wash down the airplanes at Port Koneta. He even helped the airport mechanics with some routine maintenance work, servicing the planes' cylinders, pistons, and valves.

Eventually, Neil had saved up enough money to pay for some lessons. A veteran army pilot named Aubrey Knudegard taught him. They flew in a light, high-wing monoplane called an Aeronca Champion.

Aircraft Fact File

Name:	Aeronca Champion
Nickname:	"Champ"
Length:	21.5 ft. (6.6 m)
Wingspan:	35.2 ft. (10.7 m)
Engine:	65 horsepower
Top speed:	100 mph (161 kmh)
First flight:	April 29, 1944

⋛ WALKING ON THE MOON ⋛

Buzz soon followed Neil out, and the two of them explored the lunar surface. "It has a stark beauty all its own," remarked Neil. Buzz described it as "magnificent desolation." The powdery soil was quite slippery, they discovered, but walking was no problem. They unveiled a commemorative plaque that had been mounted on *Eagle*'s base.

They planted a US flag, stiffened with wire to make it look like it was flying in a breeze. Neil photographed Buzz saluting it.

President Richard Nixon called them by radio-telephone from the White House. "This certainly has to be the most historic telephone call ever made," he said. "I just can't tell you how proud we all are of what you've done.... For one priceless moment in the whole history of man, all the people of this Earth are truly one."

Neil and Buzz spent the rest of the EVA collecting rock and soil samples and performing experiments. They set up devices to sense moonquakes and to measure the distance between the moon and Earth. Those devices would stay on the moon.

Excerpt text copyright © 2019 by Kurtis Scaletta.
Excerpt illustrations copyright © 2019 by Artful Doodlers.
Cover art copyright © 2019 by Luisa Uribe and George Ermos.
Published in the United States by Random House Children's Books,
a division of Penguin Random House LLC, New York.

>>TRAIL BLAZERS

JACKIE ROBINSON
BREAKING BARRIERS IN BASEBALL

Life is not a spectator sport.

KURTIS SCALETTA

Jackie at UCLA
1939–1941

- → **Football:** Jackie is called "the greatest ball carrier in the nation." In 1939, the Bruins go undefeated, though three games end in ties.
- → **Basketball:** Dazzling play by Jackie helps end a long losing streak by the Bruins but isn't enough to give them a winning season.
- → **Baseball:** Jackie once again plays short and gets a reputation for stealing bases but goes into a hitting slump he can't break out of.
- → **Track and Field:** Jackie sets a conference record and wins the NCAA title for the long jump.
- → **Combined:** Jackie is the first athlete at UCLA to "letter" in four sports—meaning he has significant playing time at the varsity level.

≡ LOVE AND WAR ≡

Jackie continued to shine in his second year at UCLA, but the football team and basketball team both had losing seasons. Something happened that was more important than sports or even his education. He met a student named Rachel Isum. Jackie was drawn to Rachel's intelligence and compassion.

At first, he later wrote, Jackie experienced a new kind of prejudice. Rachel Isum knew he was a star athlete and had seen him play. She was convinced he was cocky and full of himself. But as she got to know him, she learned Jackie had a serious mind and—more important—respected that she had one, too. After they'd known each other for a year, they were deeply in love.

No matter what happens, this relationship is going to be one of the most important parts of my life.

Jackie's appeal crossed color lines. Author Myron Uhlberg wrote of how his deaf father connected with Jackie because they were both out of place in the world. Bette Bao Lord wrote a fictionalized memoir called *In the Year of the Boar and Jackie Robinson*, about how Jackie's courage helped her overcome her own barriers as a Chinese immigrant. Anyone who had ever been told they didn't belong, or who stood out for their differences, felt a connection.

And some fans loved Jackie simply because he was an exciting player to watch. He would get on base, take a lead, and dare the pitcher to make a throw. He was always a threat to steal. He would steal third base with two outs. He would steal home! Some fans compared him to baseball's all-time greatest base runner, Ty Cobb. Jackie's fearlessness on the base path lifted the rest of the team. They hit better because the pitchers were rattled and infielders were distracted.

COMING SOON . . .

Simone Biles

Stephen Hawking

Martin Luther King Jr.

J. K. Rowling